THE EASY STANDARDS FAKE BOOK

Melody, Lyrics and Simplified Chords

100 Songs in the Key of "C"

ISBN-13: 978-1-4234-2515-1
ISBN-10: 1-4234-2515-4

7777 W. BLUEMOUND RD. P.O. BOX 13819 MILWAUKEE, WI 53213

For all works contained herein:
Unauthorized copying, arranging, adapting, recording or public performance is an infringement of copyright.
Infringers are liable under the law.

Visit Hal Leonard Online at
www.halleonard.com

THE EASY STANDARDS FAKE BOOK

CONTENTS

4	INTRODUCTION
5	All the Way
6	As Long As I Live
8	Between the Devil and the Deep Blue Sea
10	A Blossom Fell
12	The Blue Room
14	But Beautiful
9	C-Jam Blues
16	Caravan
18	Cherokee (Indian Love Song)
20	Come Fly with Me
22	Dancing on the Ceiling
24	Don't Explain
26	Don't Worry 'Bout Me
28	Easy Living
30	A Fine Romance
32	The Folks Who Live on the Hill
34	For All We Know
36	(I Love You) For Sentimental Reasons
38	From This Moment On
40	The Girl from Ipanema (Garôta De Ipanema)
42	Girl Talk
23	Glad to Be Unhappy
44	The Glory of Love
46	Gone with the Wind
48	Goodbye
50	Gypsy in My Soul
52	Have You Met Miss Jones?
56	Here's That Rainy Day
58	How Insensitive (Insensatez)
53	How Little We Know
60	I Ain't Got Nothin' but the Blues
62	I Don't Know Why (I Just Do)
64	I Get Along Without You Very Well (Except Sometimes)
66	I Hadn't Anyone Till You
68	I Let a Song Go Out of My Heart
70	I Wanna Be Loved
72	I Will Wait for You
74	I Won't Dance
76	I'll Take Romance
78	I'm a Fool to Want You
80	I'm Confessin' (That I Love You)
82	I'm Old Fashioned
84	If I Should Lose You
86	Imagination
63	In a Mellow Tone
88	In Love in Vain
90	Is You Is, Or Is You Ain't (Ma' Baby)
92	It Don't Mean a Thing (If It Ain't Got That Swing)
94	It's a Blue World
96	It's a Good Day
98	It's Easy to Remember
100	Just One More Chance
102	The Lady Is a Tramp

104 The Lady's in Love with You	162 Shall We Dance?
106 Learnin' the Blues	164 So Nice (Summer Samba)
108 Let There Be You	131 Some Day My Prince Will Come
110 Let's Fall in Love	166 A Sunday Kind of Love
111 Like Someone in Love	168 The Surrey with the Fringe on Top
112 Little Girl Blue	170 There Will Never Be Another You
114 Love You Madly	167 Time After Time
113 A Lovely Way to Spend an Evening	172 Up with the Lark
116 Lullaby of the Leaves	174 The Way You Look Tonight
118 The Man That Got Away	176 Witchcraft
120 Meditation (Meditacão)	178 Wives and Lovers (Hey, Little Girl)
122 More Than You Know	180 Wrap Your Troubles in Dreams (And Dream Your Troubles Away)
124 My Ideal	
125 My Lucky Star	186 Yesterdays
126 My Old Flame	182 You Are Too Beautiful
128 My One and Only Love	184 You Brought a New Kind of Love to Me
130 My Shining Hour	187 CHORD SPELLER
132 Nancy – With the Laughing Face	
134 The Nearness of You	
136 Never Let Me Go	
138 A Nightingale Sang in Berkeley Square	
140 One for My Baby (And One More for the Road)	
142 One Morning in May	
144 One Note Samba (Samba De Uma Nota So)	
146 Only Trust Your Heart	
148 The Other Side of the Tracks	
150 Out of Nowhere	
152 Pick Yourself Up	
154 Polka Dots and Moonbeams	
156 Prelude to a Kiss	
158 Quiet Nights of Quiet Stars (Corcovado)	
160 Real Live Girl	

INTRODUCTION

What Is a Fake Book?

A fake book has one-line music notation consisting of melody, lyrics and chord symbols. This lead sheet format is a "musical shorthand" which is an invaluable resource for all musicians—hobbyists to professionals.

Here's how *The Easy Standards Fake Book* differs from most standard fake books:

- All songs are in the key of C.

- Many of the melodies have been simplified.

- Only five basic chord types are used—major, minor, seventh, diminished and augmented.

- The music notation is larger for ease of reading.

In the event that you haven't used chord symbols to create accompaniment, or your experience is limited, a chord speller chart is included at the back of the book to help you get started.

Have fun!

AS LONG AS I LIVE

© 1934 (Renewed 1962) FRED AHLERT MUSIC GROUP,
TED KOEHLER MUSIC CO. and S.A. MUSIC CO.
All Rights for FRED AHLERT MUSIC GROUP and TED KOEHLER MUSIC CO.
Administered by BUG MUSIC
All Rights Reserved   Used by Permission

Lyric by TED KOEHLER
Music by HAROLD ARLEN

Moderately

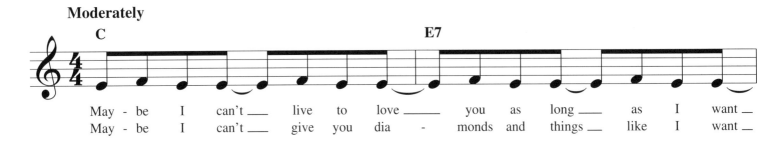

May-be I can't ___ live to love ___ you as long ___ as I want
May-be I can't ___ give you dia-monds and things ___ like I want

___ to,   life is-n't long e-nough,
___ to,   but I can prom-ise you,

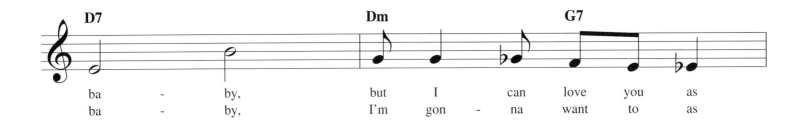

ba - by,   but I can love you as
ba - by,   I'm gon-na want to as

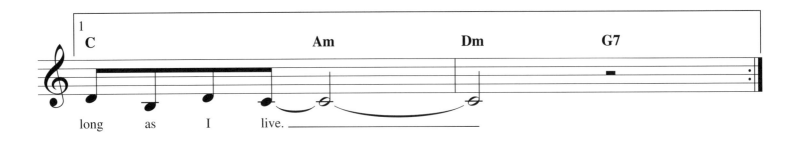

long as I live.

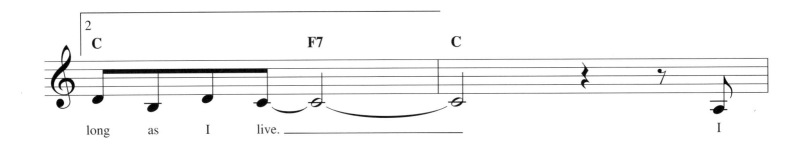

long as I live. ___ I

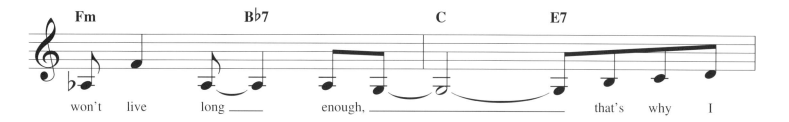
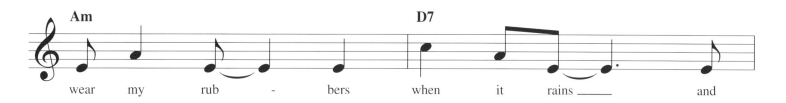
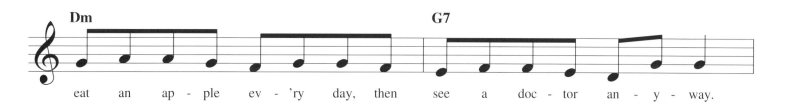

C-JAM BLUES

Copyright © 1942 (Renewed 1969) by Famous Music LLC in the U.S.A.
Rights for the world outside the U.S.A. Controlled by EMI Robbins Catalog Inc. (Publishing)
and Warner Bros. Publications U.S. Inc. (Print)
International Copyright Secured   All Rights Reserved

By DUKE ELLINGTON

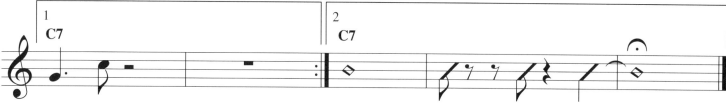

A Blossom Fell

Copyright © 1954, 1955 John Fields Music Co. Ltd., London, England
Copyright Renewed and Assigned to Shapiro, Bernstein & Co., Inc., New York
  for U.S.A. and Canada
International Copyright Secured   All Rights Reserved
Used by Permission

Words and Music by HOWARD BARNES,
HAROLD CORNELIUS and DOMINIC JOHN

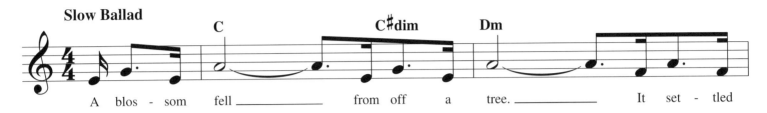

A blos - som fell ____ from off a tree. ____ It set - tled

soft - ly on the lips you turned to me. ____ The gyp - sies

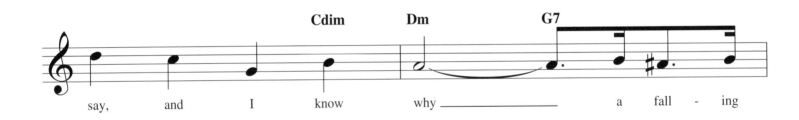

say, and I know why ____ a fall - ing

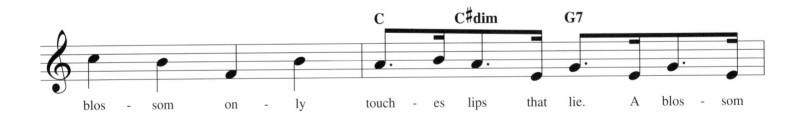

blos - som on - ly touch - es lips that lie. A blos - som

fell ____ and ver - y soon ____ I saw you

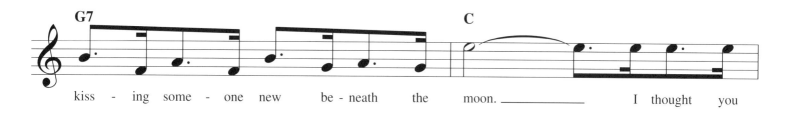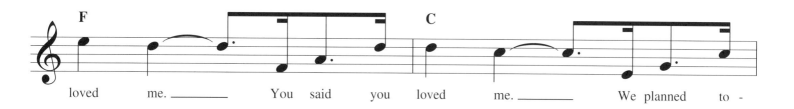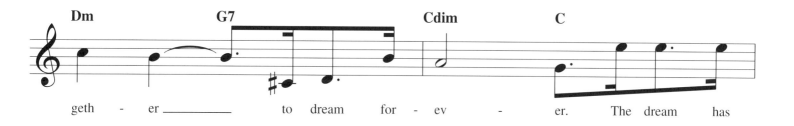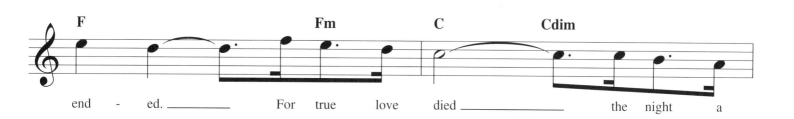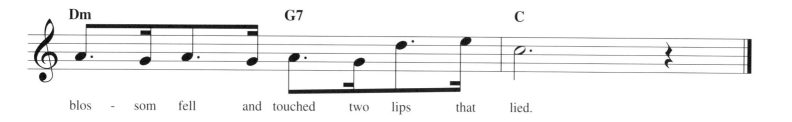

THE BLUE ROOM
from THE GIRL FRIEND

Copyright © 1926 (Renewed) by Chappell & Co.
Rights for the Extended Renewal Term in the U.S.
 Controlled by Williamson Music and WB Music Corp. o/b/o The Estate Of Lorenz Hart
International Copyright Secured   All Rights Reserved

Words by LORENZ HART
Music by RICHARD RODGERS

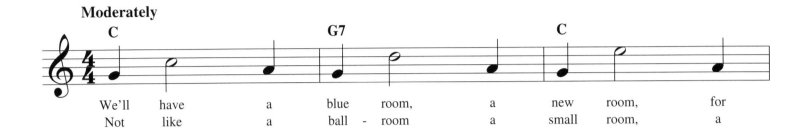

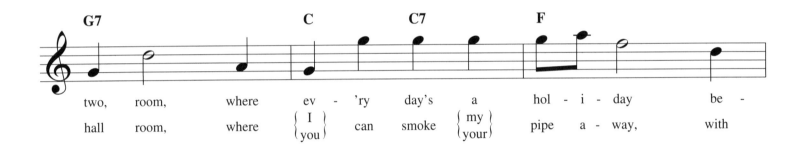

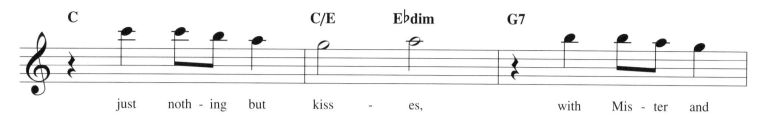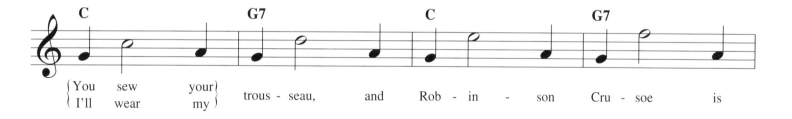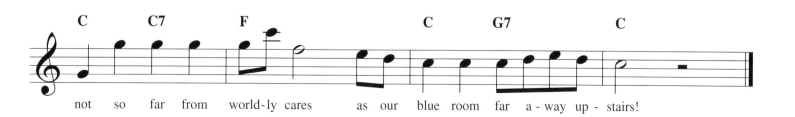

BUT BEAUTIFUL
from ROAD TO RIO

Words by JOHNNY BURKE
Music by JIMMY VAN HEUSEN

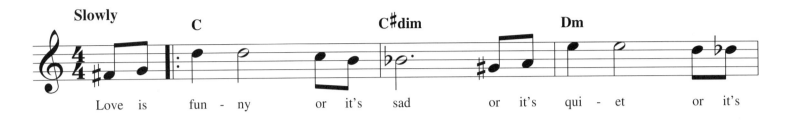

Love is fun-ny or it's sad or it's qui-et or it's

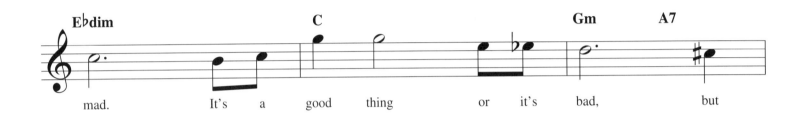

mad. It's a good thing or it's bad, but

beau-ti-ful! Beau-ti-ful to take a chance and

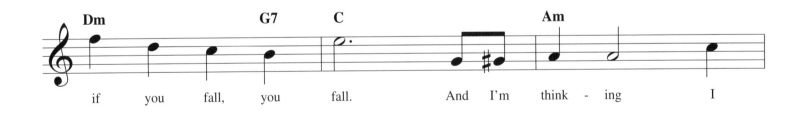

if you fall, you fall. And I'm think-ing I

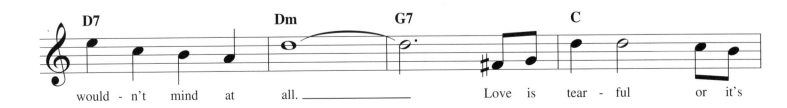

would-n't mind at all. Love is tear-ful or it's

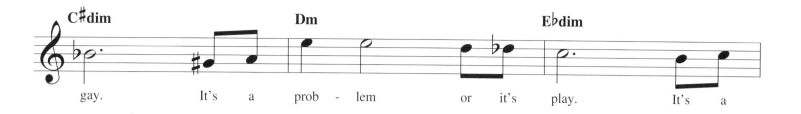

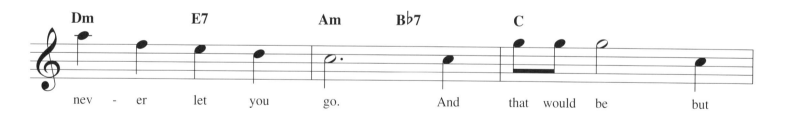
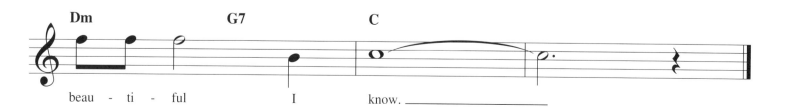

CARAVAN
from SOPHISTICATED LADIES

Words and Music by DUKE ELLINGTON, IRVING MILLS and JUAN TIZOL

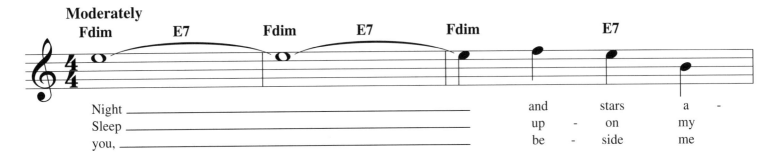
Night ____ and stars a-
Sleep ____ up-on my
you, ____ be-side me

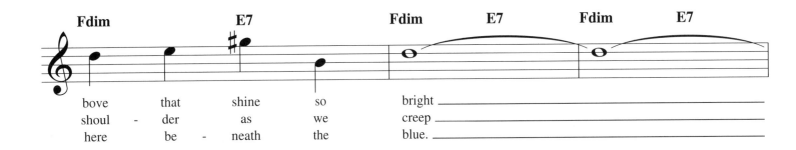
bove that shine so bright ____
shoul-der as we creep ____
here be-neath the blue. ____

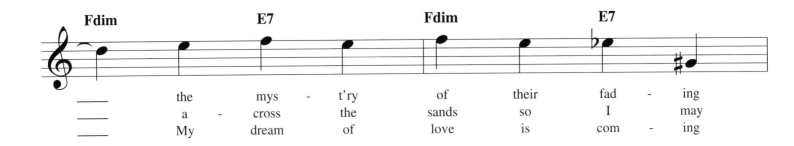
____ the mys-t'ry of their fad-ing
____ a-cross the sands so I may
____ My dream of love is com-ing

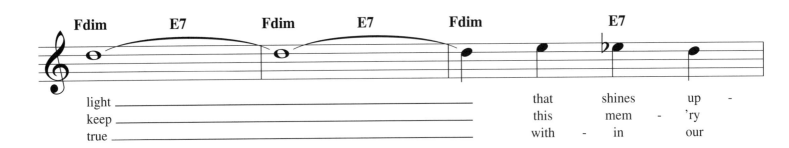
light ____ that shines up-
keep ____ this mem-'ry
true ____ with-in our

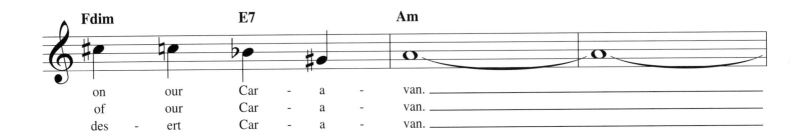
on our Car-a-van. ____
of our Car-a-van. ____
des-ert Car-a-van. ____

17

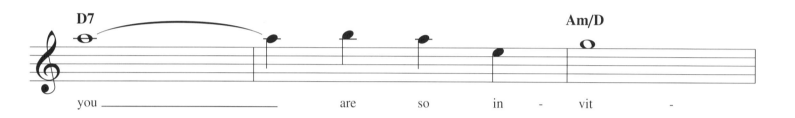
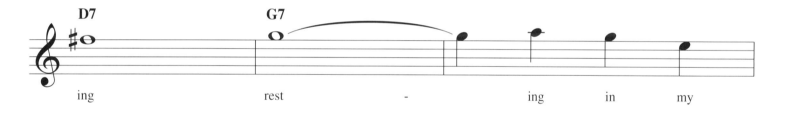

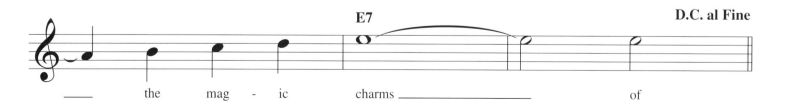

CHEROKEE
(Indian Love Song)

Copyright © 1938 The Peter Maurice Music Co., Ltd., London, England
Copyright Renewed and Assigned to Shapiro, Bernstein & Co., Inc., New York
  for U.S.A. and Canada
International Copyright Secured   All Rights Reserved
Used by Permission

Words and Music by
RAY NOBLE

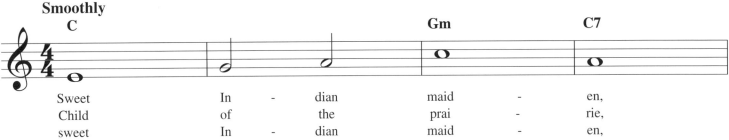

Sweet   In - dian   maid - en,
Child   of the   prai - rie,
sweet   In - dian   maid - en,

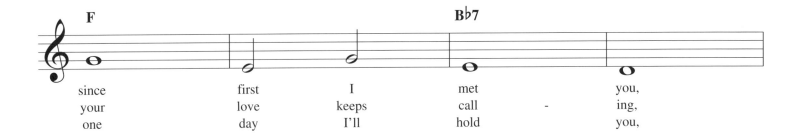

since   first   I   met   you,
your   love   keeps call - ing,
one   day   I'll hold   you,

I   can't   for - get   you,
my   heart   en - thrall - ing,
in   my   arms fold   you,

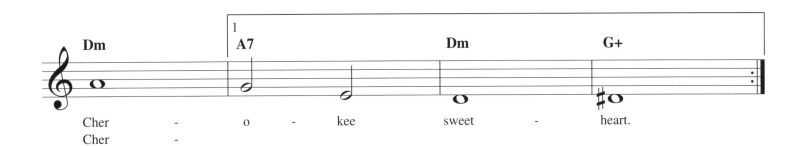

Cher - o - kee   sweet - heart.
Cher -

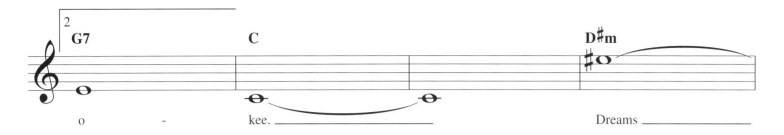

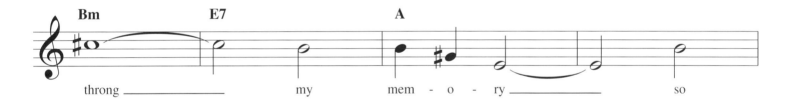

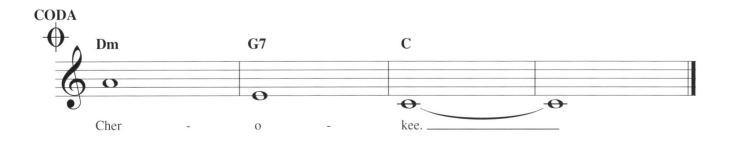

COME FLY WITH ME

Words by SAMMY CAHN
Music by JAMES VAN HEUSEN

Come fly with me! Let's fly! Let's fly a - way!
fly with me! Let's float down to Pe - ru!

If you can use some ex - o - tic booze, there's a
In Lla - ma Land there's a one - man band and he'll

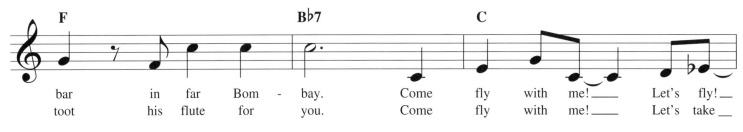

bar in far Bom - bay. Come fly with me! Let's fly!
toot his flute for you. Come fly with me! Let's take

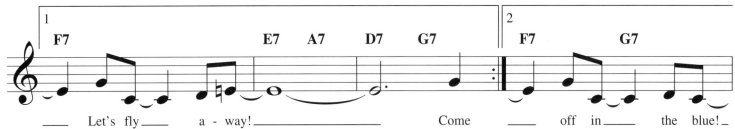

Let's fly a - way! Come off in the blue!

Once I get you up there, where the air is

rar - i - fied, we'll just glide,

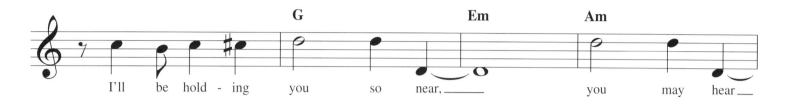

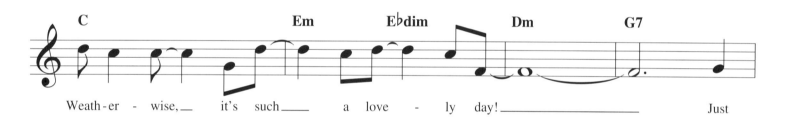
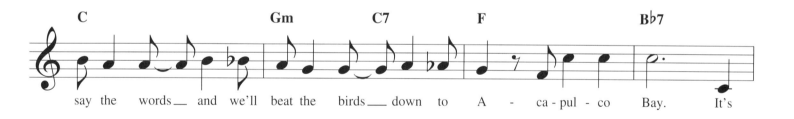
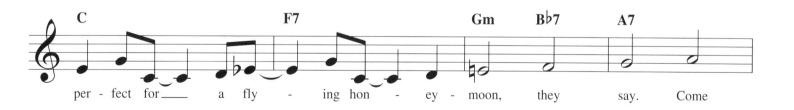
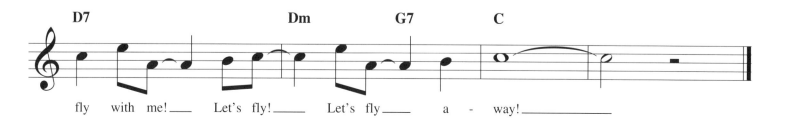

Dancing on the Ceiling

from SIMPLE SIMON
from EVER GREEN

Words by Lorenz Hart
Music by Richard Rodgers

Copyright © 1931 (Renewed) by Chappell & Co.
Rights for the Extended Renewal Term in the U.S. Controlled by
Williamson Music and WB Music Corp. o/b/o The Estate Of Lorenz Hart
International Copyright Secured   All Rights Reserved

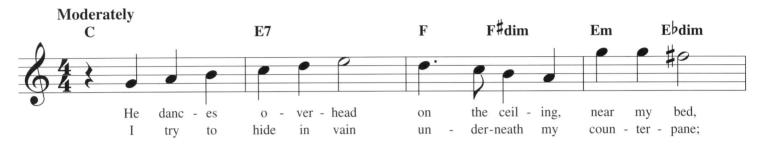
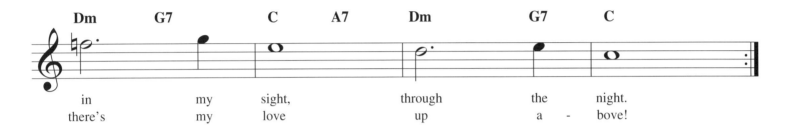

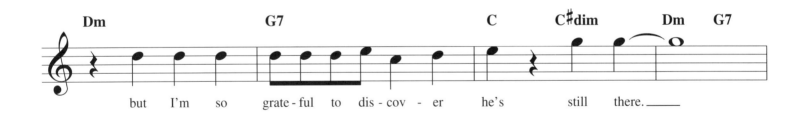
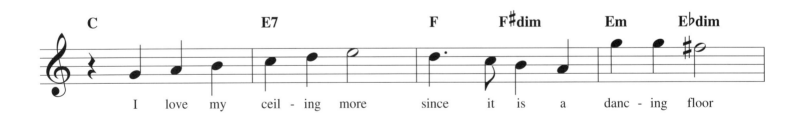
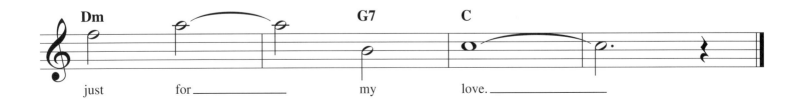

GLAD TO BE UNHAPPY
from ON YOUR TOES

Words by LORENZ HART
Music by RICHARD RODGERS

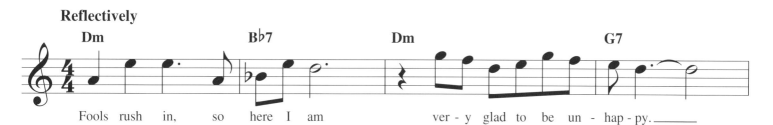
Fools rush in, so here I am ver-y glad to be un-hap-py.

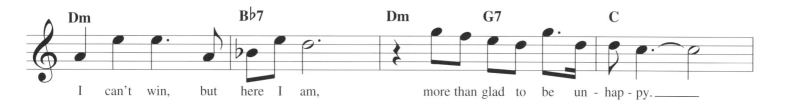
I can't win, but here I am, more than glad to be un-hap-py.

Un-re-quit-ed love's a bore, and I've got it pret-ty bad.

But for some-one you a-dore, it's a pleas-ure to be sad.

Like a stray-ing ba-by lamb, with no mam-my and no pap-py, I'm so un-

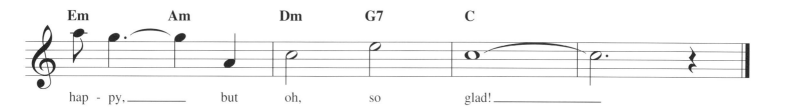
hap-py, but oh, so glad!

DON'T EXPLAIN

Words and Music by BILLIE HOLIDAY
and ARTHUR HERZOG

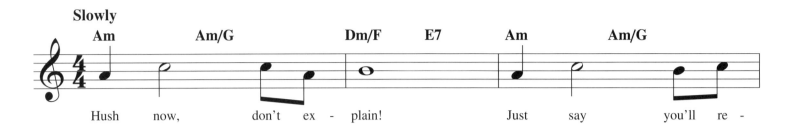
Hush now, don't ex - plain! Just say you'll re -

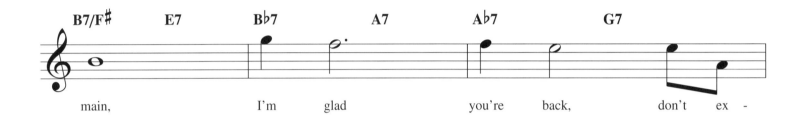
main, I'm glad you're back, don't ex -

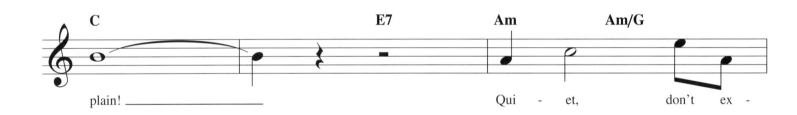
plain! Qui - et, don't ex -

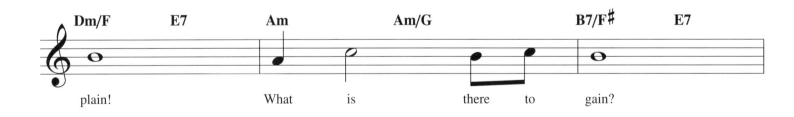
plain! What is there to gain?

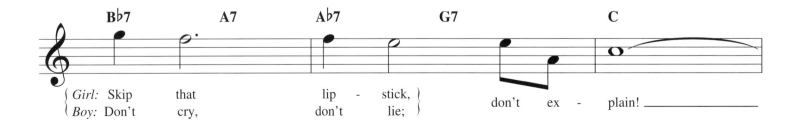
{ Girl: Skip that lip - stick, }
{ Boy: Don't cry, don't lie; } don't ex - plain!

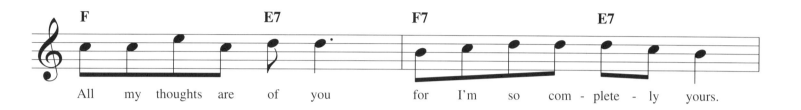
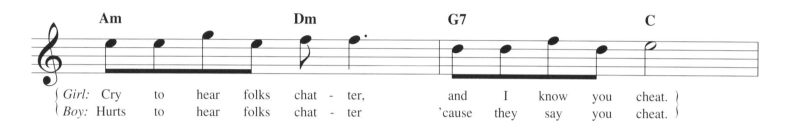

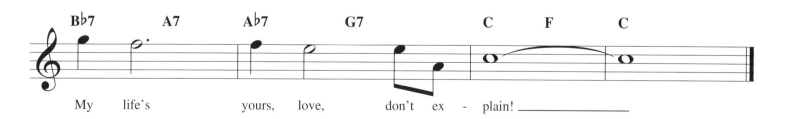

DON'T WORRY 'BOUT ME
from COTTON CLUB PARADE

Lyric by TED KOEHLER
Music by RUBE BLOOM

© 1939 (Renewed 1967) FRED AHLERT MUSIC GROUP (ASCAP),
TED KOEHLER MUSIC CO. (ASCAP)/Administered by BUG MUSIC and EMI MILLS MUSIC INC.
All Rights Reserved   Used by Permission

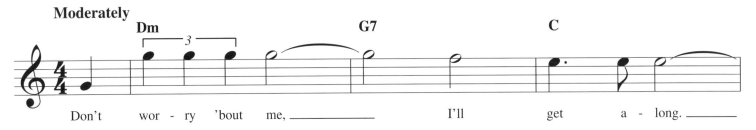
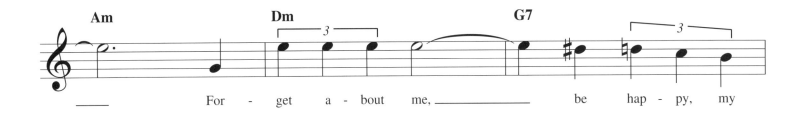

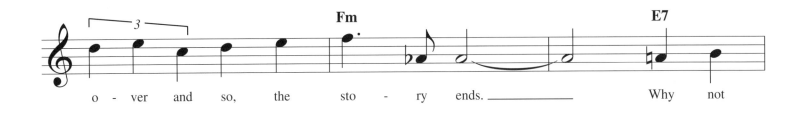
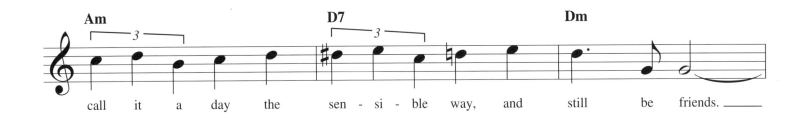

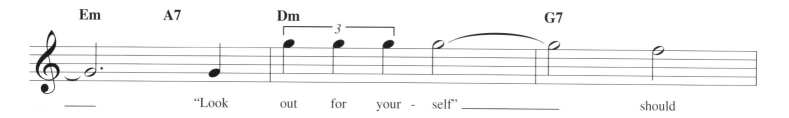

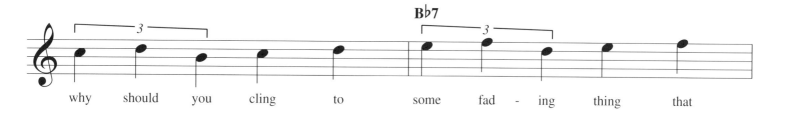
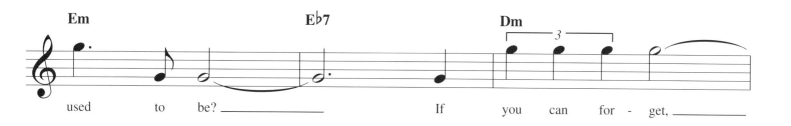
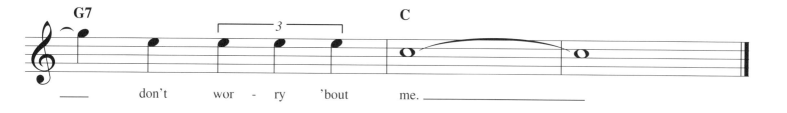

EASY LIVING
Theme from the Paramount Picture EASY LIVING

Words and Music by LEO ROBIN and RALPH RAINGER

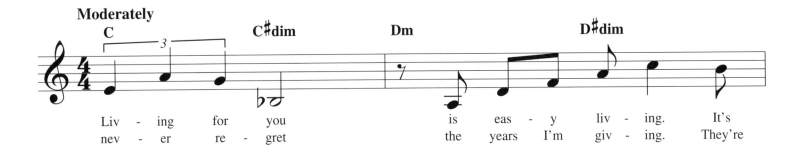

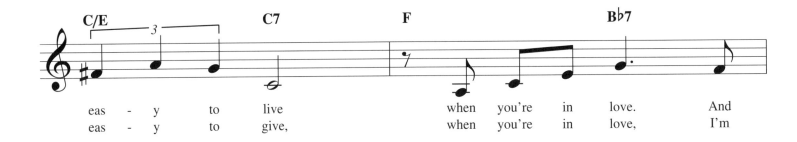

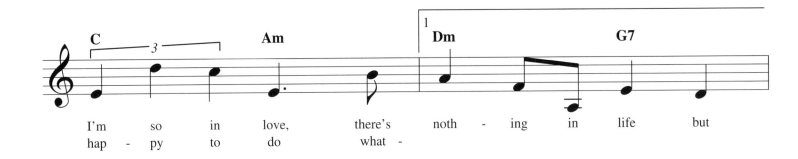

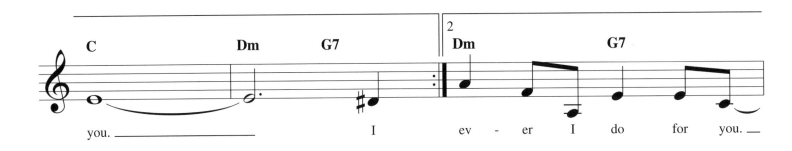

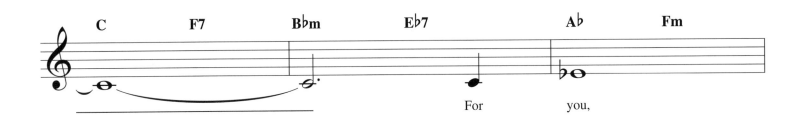

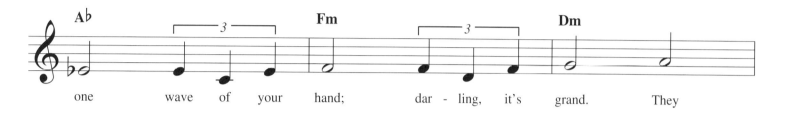
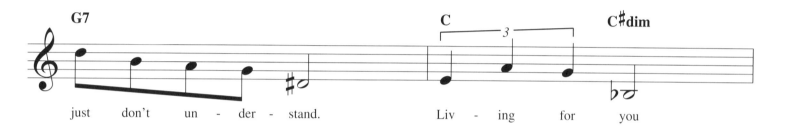

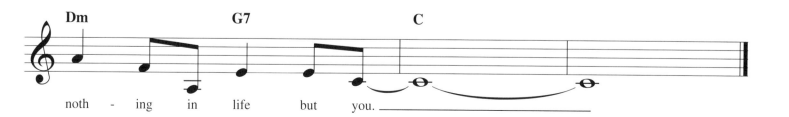

A FINE ROMANCE
from SWING TIME

Words by DOROTHY FIELDS
Music by JEROME KERN

Copyright © 1936 UNIVERSAL - POLYGRAM INTERNATIONAL PUBLISHING, INC. and ALDI MUSIC
Copyright Renewed
Print Rights for ALDI MUSIC in the U.S. Controlled and Administered by HAPPY ASPEN MUSIC LLC
c/o SHAPIRO, BERNSTEIN & CO., INC.
All Rights Reserved   Used by Permission

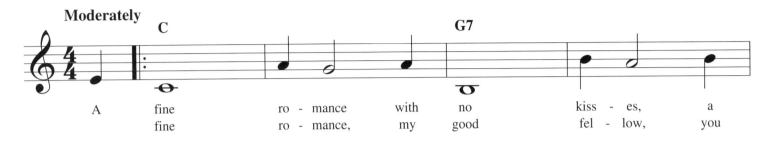
A fine ro - mance with no kiss - es, a
fine ro - mance, my good fel - low, you

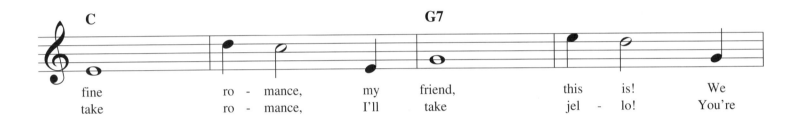
fine ro - mance, my friend, this is! We
take ro - mance, I'll take jel - lo! You're

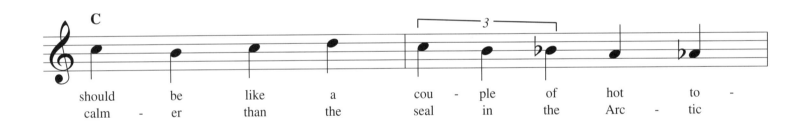
should be like a cou - ple of hot to -
calm - er than the seal in the Arc - tic

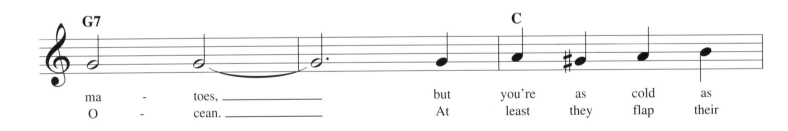
ma - toes, but you're as cold as
O - cean. At least they flap their

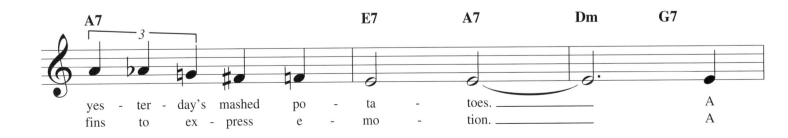
yes - ter - day's mashed po - ta - toes. A
fins to ex - press e - mo - tion. A

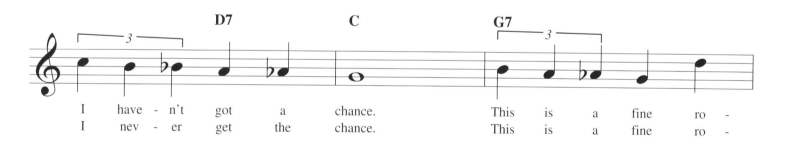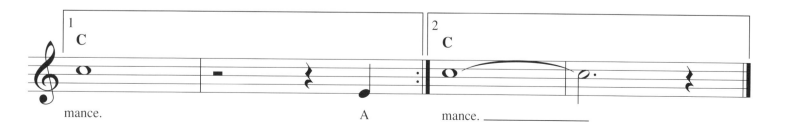

THE FOLKS WHO LIVE ON THE HILL
from HIGH, WIDE AND HANDSOME

Lyric by OSCAR HAMMERSTEIN II
Music by JEROME KERN

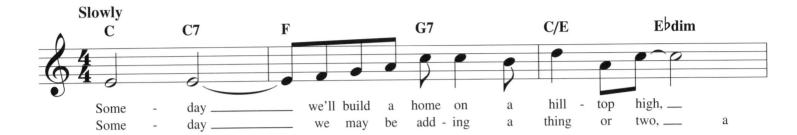
Some - day _____ we'll build a home on a hill - top high, _____
Some - day _____ we may be add - ing a thing or two, _____ a

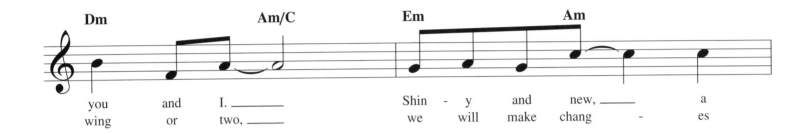
you and I. _____ Shin - y and new, _____ a
wing or two, _____ we will make chang - es

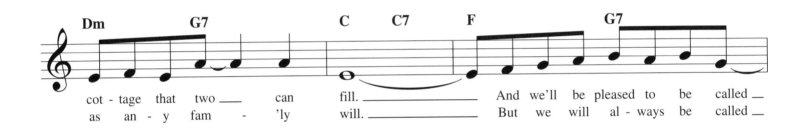
cot - tage that two _____ can fill. _____ And we'll be pleased to be called _____
as an - y fam - 'ly will. _____ But we will al - ways be called _____

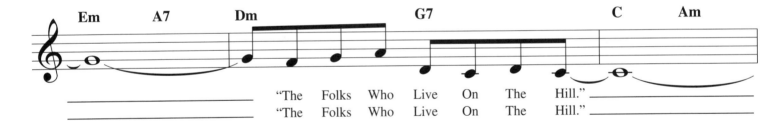
"The Folks Who Live On The Hill." _____
"The Folks Who Live On The Hill." _____

Our _____ ve - ran - da will com - mand a view of mead - ows

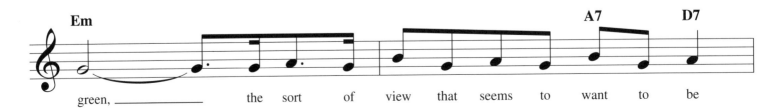
green, _____ the sort of view that seems to want to be

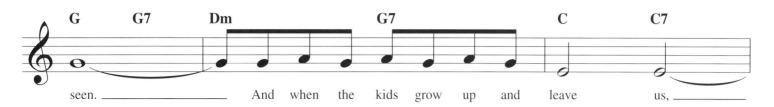
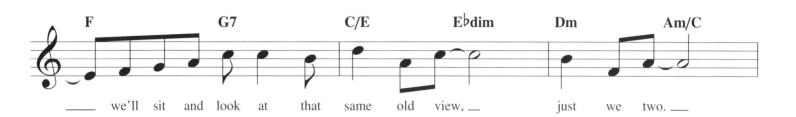
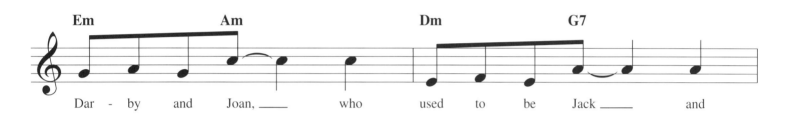
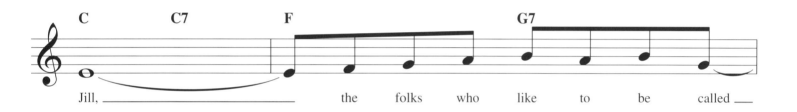

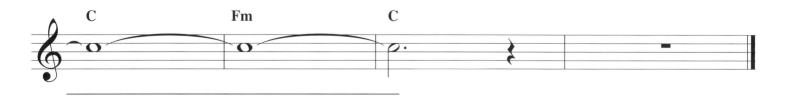

FOR ALL WE KNOW

Words by SAM M. LEWIS
Music by J. FRED COOTS

TRO - © Copyright 1934 (Renewed) and 1956 (Renewed) Cromwell Music, Inc.,
New York, NY and Toy Town Tunes, Inc., Boca Raton, FL
International Copyright Secured
All Rights Reserved Including Public Performance For Profit
Used by Permission

For all we know we may nev-er meet a-gain.

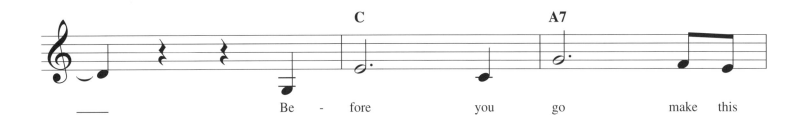

Be - fore you go make this

mo - ment sweet a - gain. We won't say good -

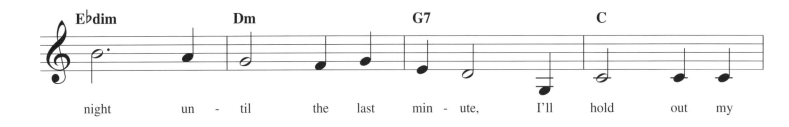

night un - til the last min - ute, I'll hold out my

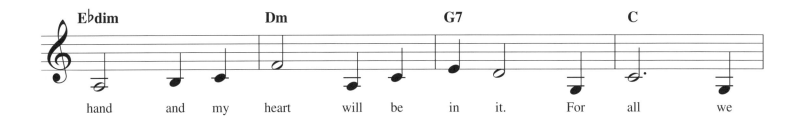

hand and my heart will be in it. For all we

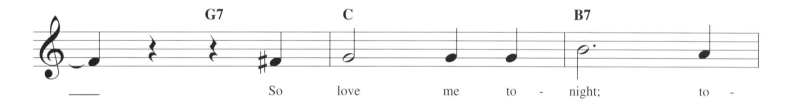

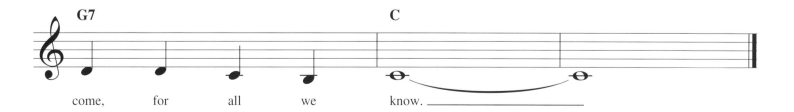

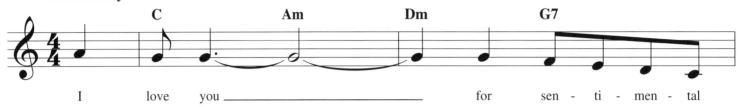

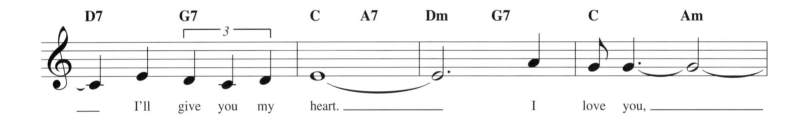

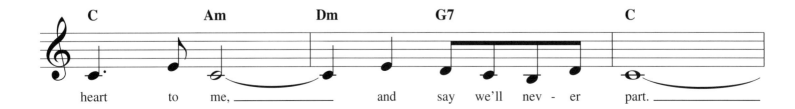

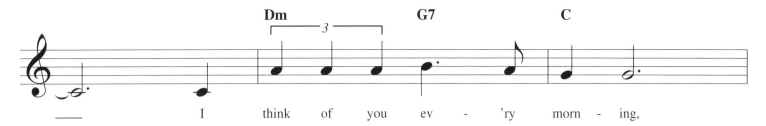
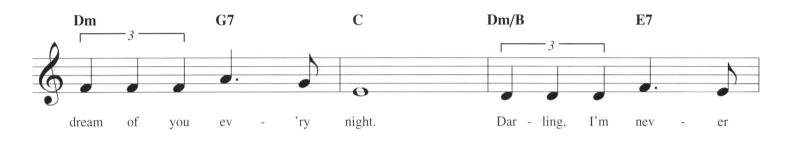
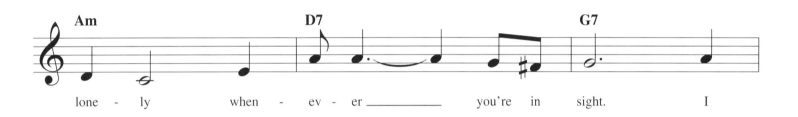
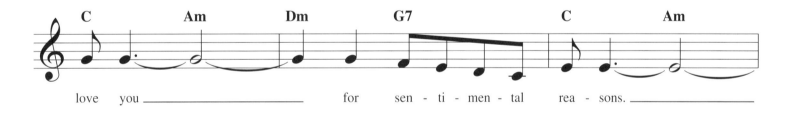

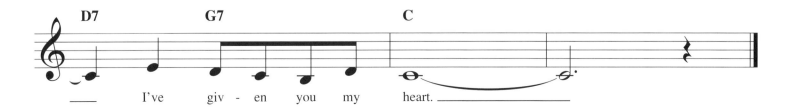

FROM THIS MOMENT ON
from OUT OF THIS WORLD

Copyright © 1950 by Cole Porter
Copyright Renewed, Assigned to Robert H. Montgomery, Trustee of the
   Cole Porter Musical and Literary Property Trusts
Chappell & Co. owner of publication and allied rights throughout the world
International Copyright Secured   All Rights Reserved

Words and Music by
COLE PORTER

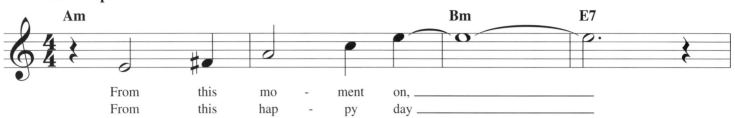

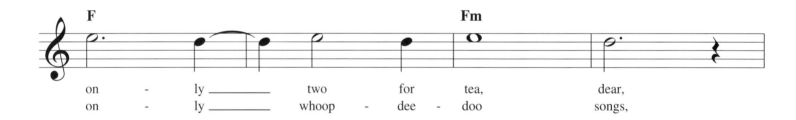

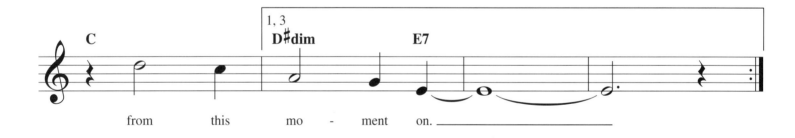

THE GIRL FROM IPANEMA
(Garôta De Ipanema)

Music by ANTONIO CARLOS JOBIM
English Words by NORMAN GIMBEL
Original Words by VINICIUS DE MORAES

Copyright © 1963 ANTONIO CARLOS JOBIM and VINICIUS DE MORAES, Brazil
Copyright Renewed 1991 and Assigned to SONGS OF UNIVERSAL, INC. and NEW THUNDER MUSIC, INC.
English Words Renewed 1991 by NORMAN GIMBEL for the World and Assigned to NEW THUNDER MUSIC, INC.
Administered by GIMBEL MUSIC GROUP, INC. (P.O. Box 15221, Beverly Hills, CA 90209-1221 USA)
All Rights Reserved   Used by Permission

Moderate Bossa Nova

Tall and tan and young and love-ly, the girl from I- pa- ne-
When she walks she's like a sam- ba that swings so cool and sways

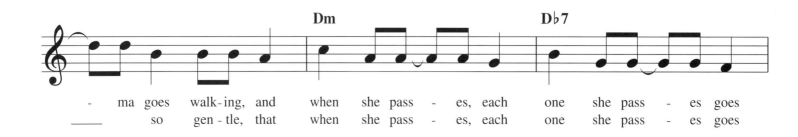

-ma goes walk-ing, and when she pass- es, each one she pass- es goes
____ so gen- tle, that when she pass- es, each one she pass- es goes

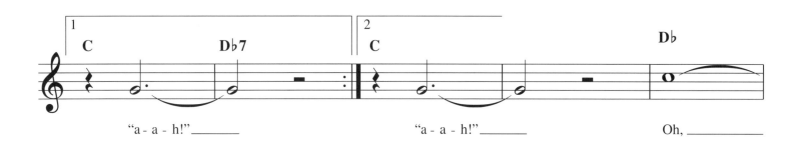

"a- a- h!"____   "a- a- h!"____   Oh,____

____ but I watch her so sad- ly. ____   How ____

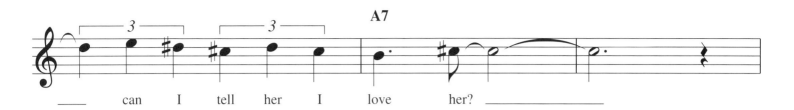

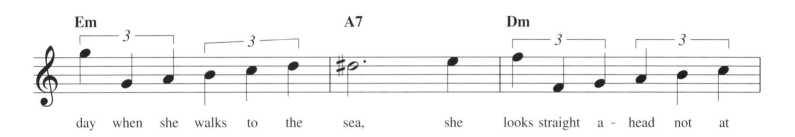

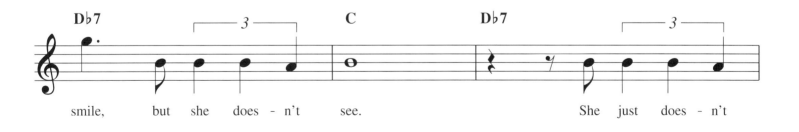
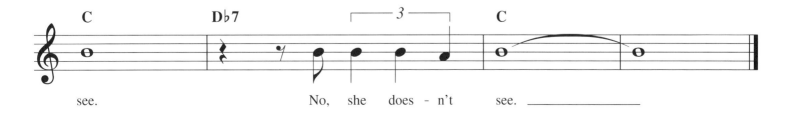

GIRL TALK
from the Paramount Picture HARLOW

Words by BOBBY TROUP
Music by NEAL HEFTI

{They/We} like to chat about the dress-es {they/we} will wear to-night.

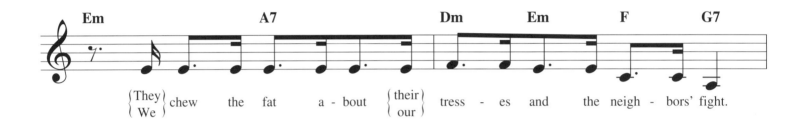
{They/We} chew the fat about {their/our} tress-es and the neigh-bors' fight.

In-con-se-quen-tial things that men don't real-ly care to know

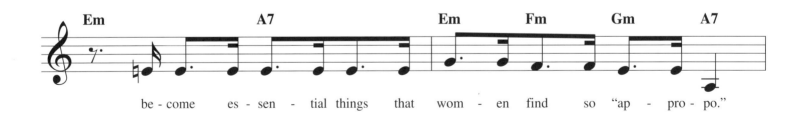
be-come es-sen-tial things that wom-en find so "ap-ro-po."

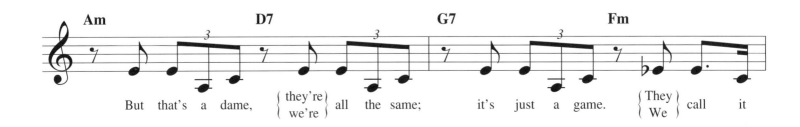
But that's a dame, {they're/we're} all the same; it's just a game. {They/We} call it

THE GLORY OF LOVE
from GUESS WHO'S COMING TO DINNER

Copyright © 1936 Shapiro, Bernstein & Co., Inc., New York
Copyright Renewed
International Copyright Secured   All Rights Reserved
Used by Permission

Words and Music by
BILLY HILL

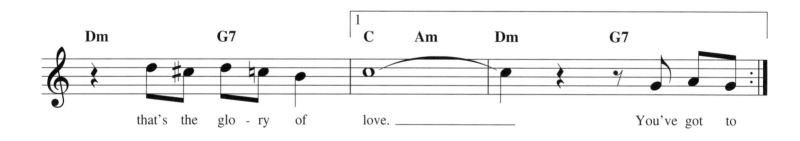

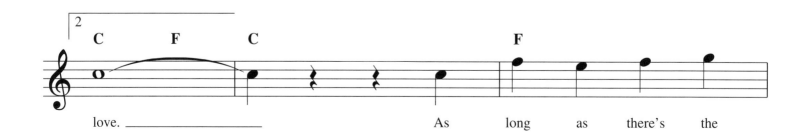

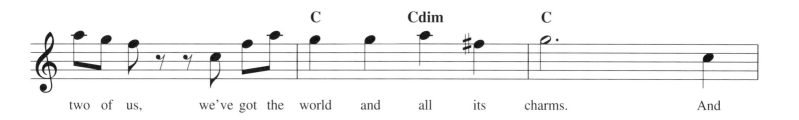

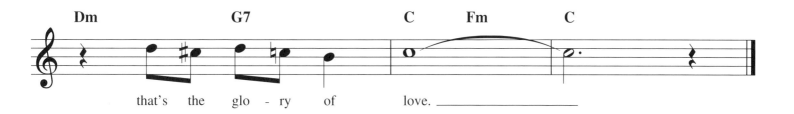

Gone with the Wind

Words and Music by HERB MAGIDSON and ALLIE WRUBEL

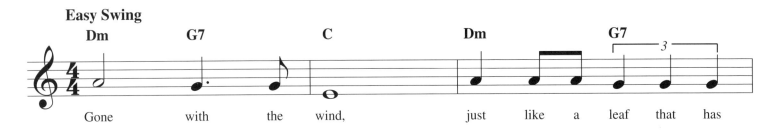
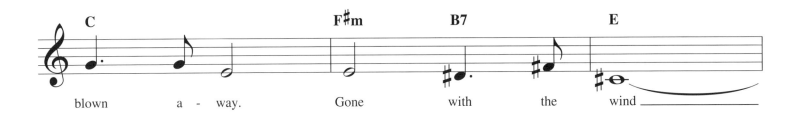
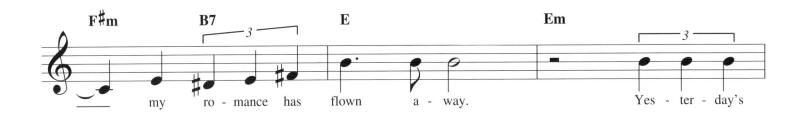
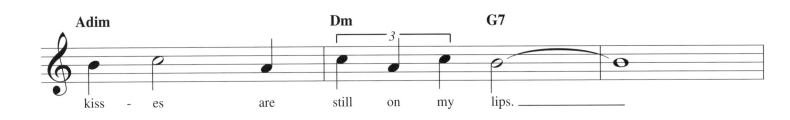
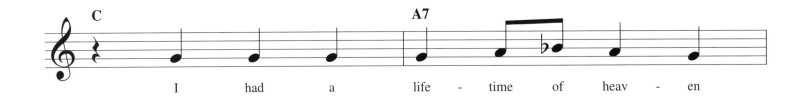

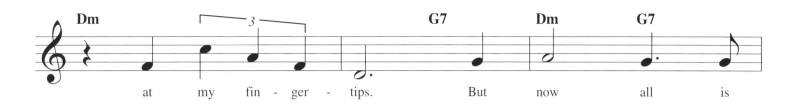
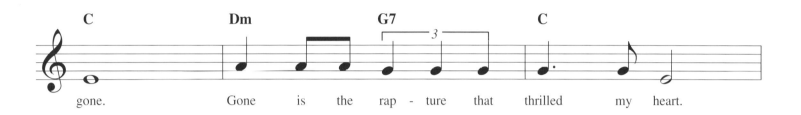
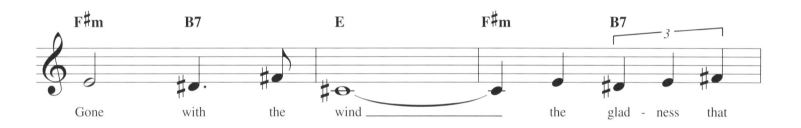
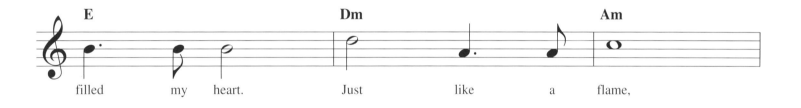

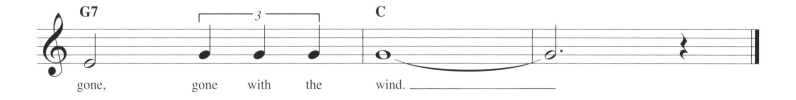

GOODBYE

Words and Music by
GORDON JENKINS

Copyright © 1935 LaSALLE MUSIC PUBLISHING, INC.
Copyright Renewed, Assigned to UNIVERSAL MUSIC CORP.
All Rights Reserved   Used by Permission

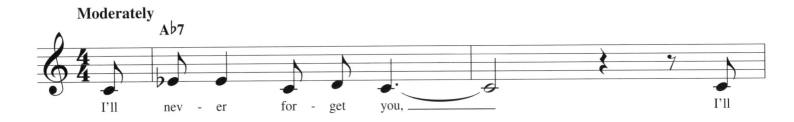

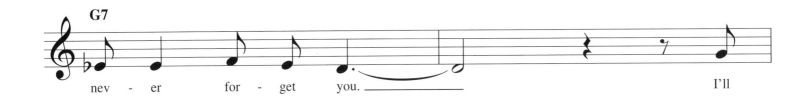

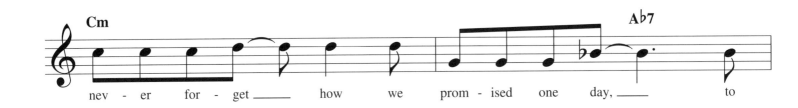

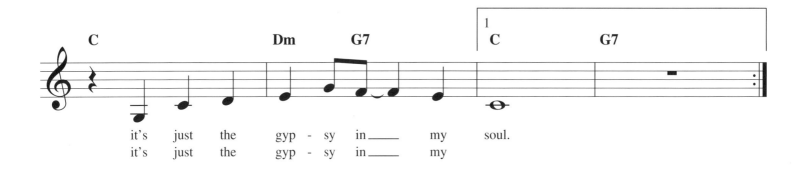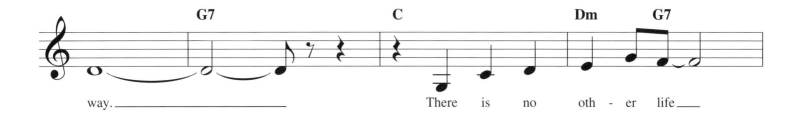

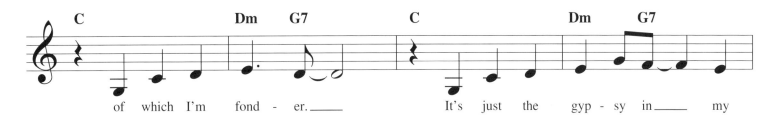

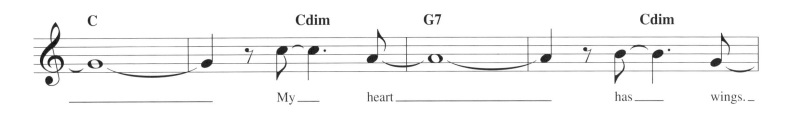
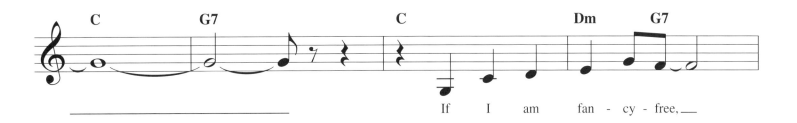

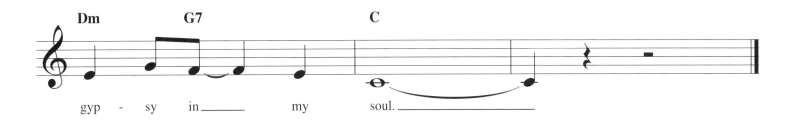

HAVE YOU MET MISS JONES?
from I'D RATHER BE RIGHT

Words by LORENZ HART
Music by RICHARD RODGERS

Copyright © 1937 (Renewed) by Chappell & Co.
Rights for the Extended Renewal Term in the U.S. Controlled by Williamson Music
and WB Music Corp. o/b/o The Estate of Lorenz Hart
International Copyright Secured   All Rights Reserved

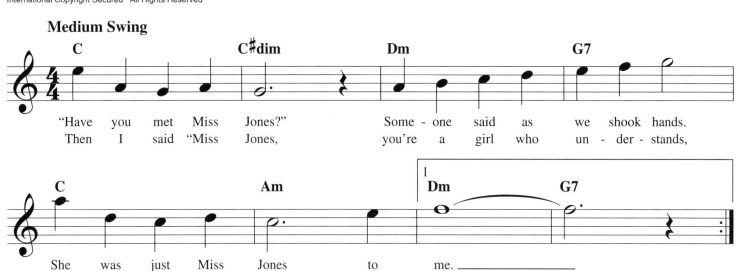

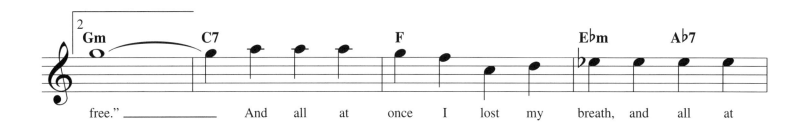

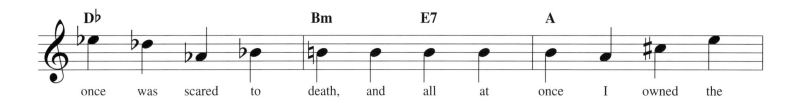

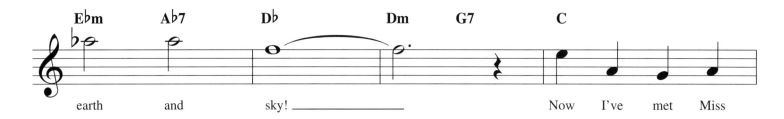

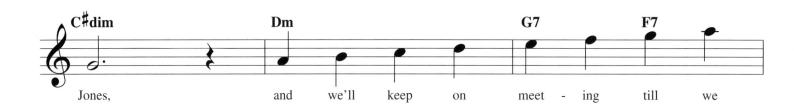

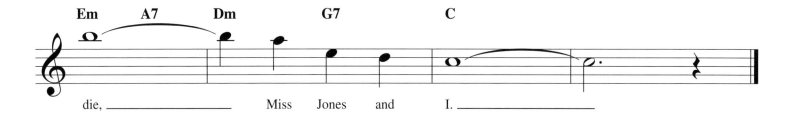

HOW LITTLE WE KNOW

Words and Music by HOAGY CARMICHAEL and JOHNNY MERCER

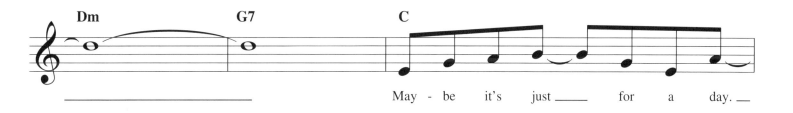
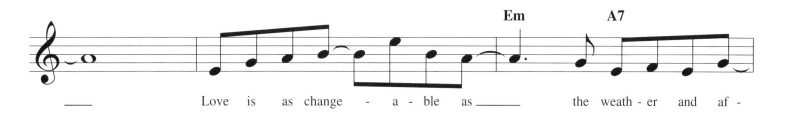
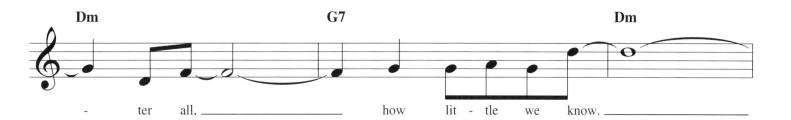

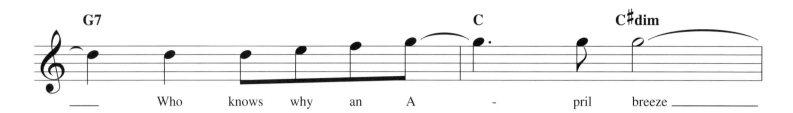
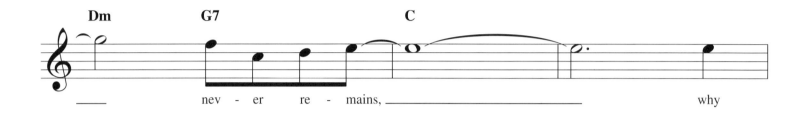
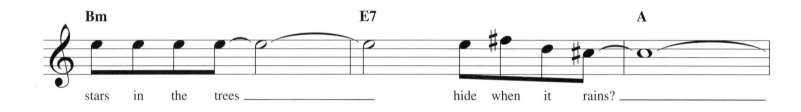

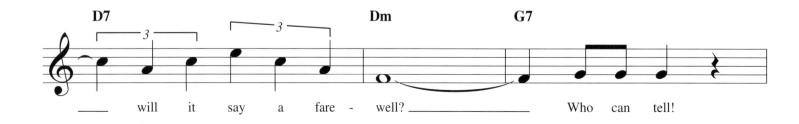

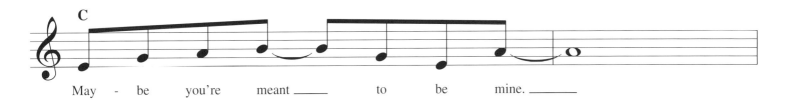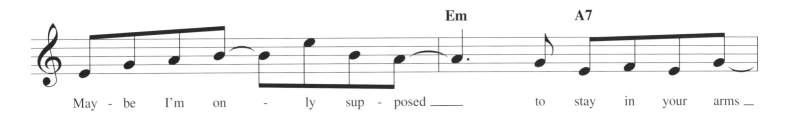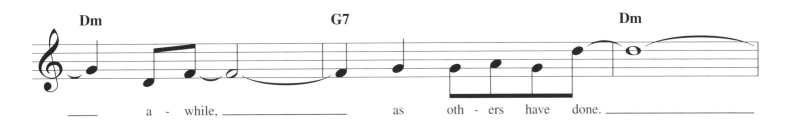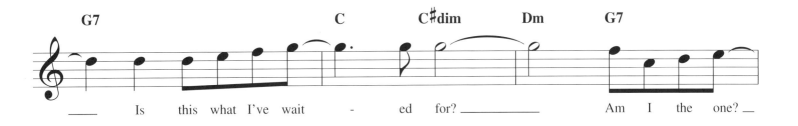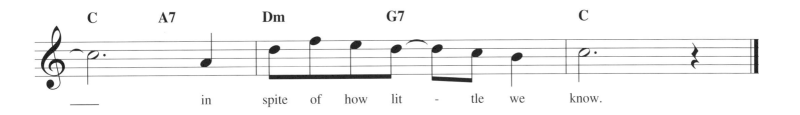

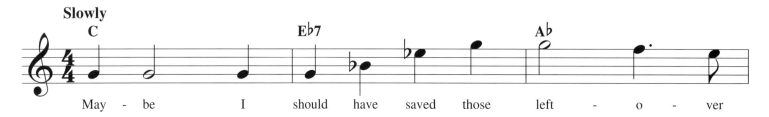
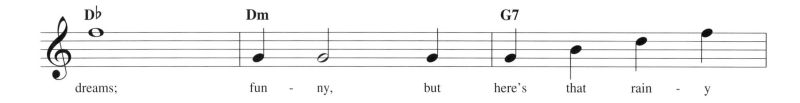
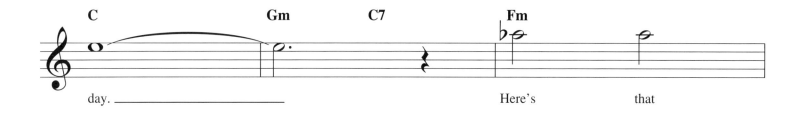
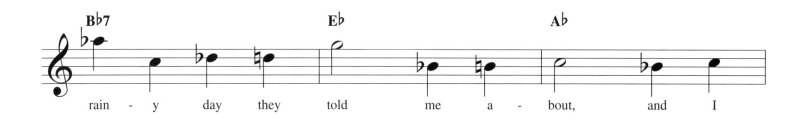

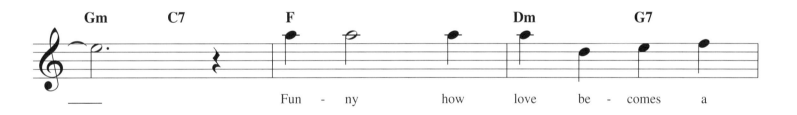

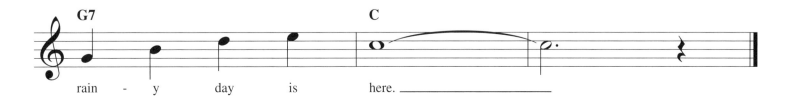

HOW INSENSITIVE
(Insensatez)

Music by ANTONIO CARLOS JOBIM
Original Words by VINICIUS DE MORAES
English Words by NORMAN GIMBEL

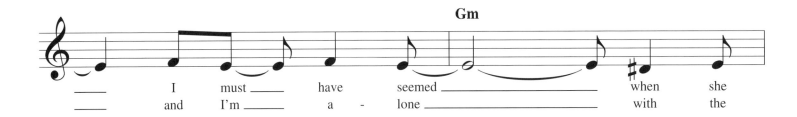
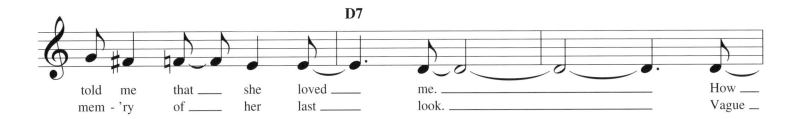

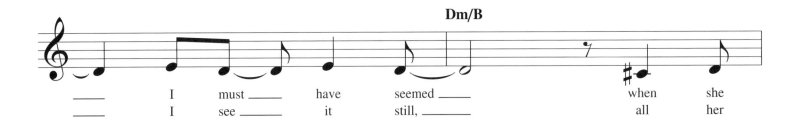
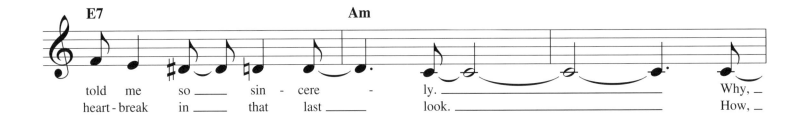

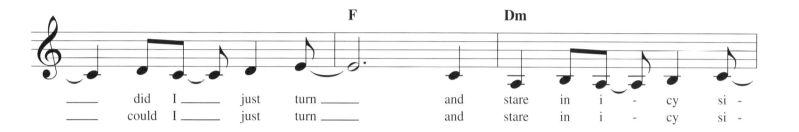
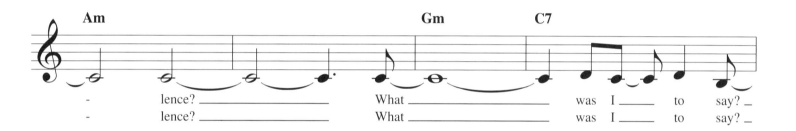

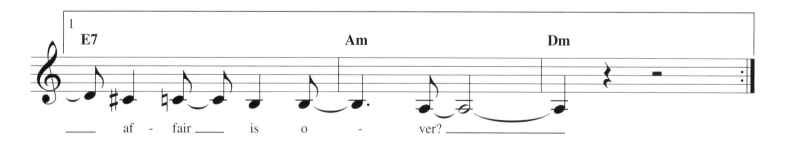
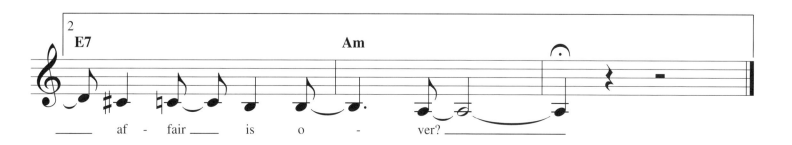

I AIN'T GOT NOTHIN' BUT THE BLUES

Words by DON GEORGE
Music by DUKE ELLINGTON

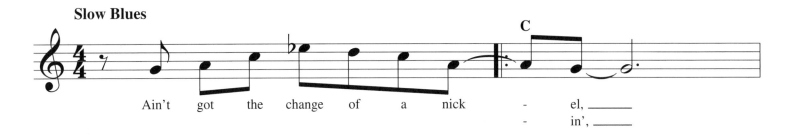
Slow Blues
Ain't got the change of a nick - el, _____

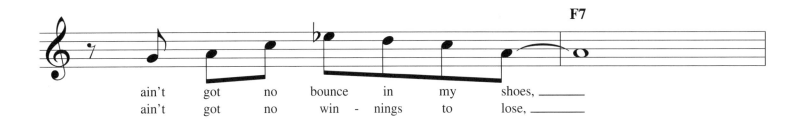
ain't got no bounce in my shoes, _____
ain't got no win - nings to lose, _____

ain't got no fan - cy to tick - le, _____
ain't got a dream that is work - in', _____

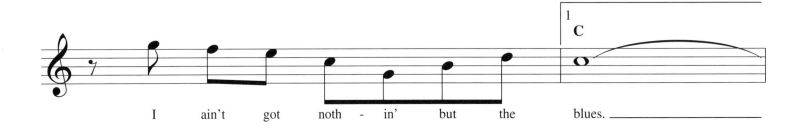
I ain't got noth - in' but the blues.

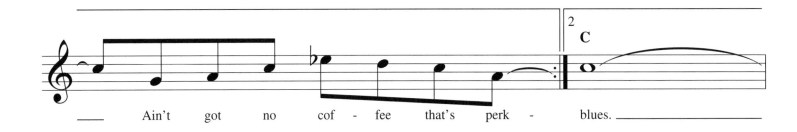
_____ Ain't got no cof - fee that's perk - blues.

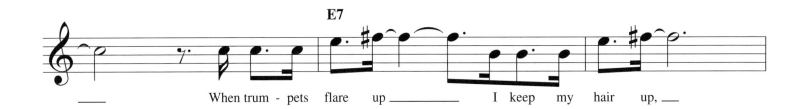
When trum - pets flare up _____ I keep my hair up, _____

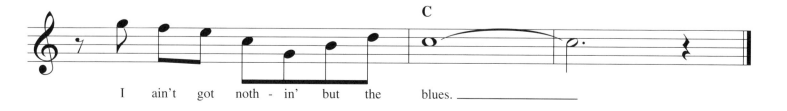

I DON'T KNOW WHY
(I Just Do)

Lyric by ROY TURK
Music by FRED E. AHLERT

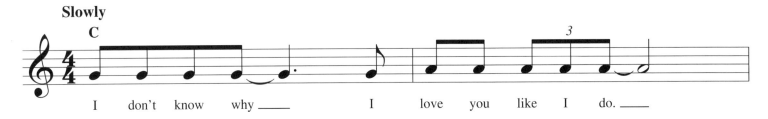
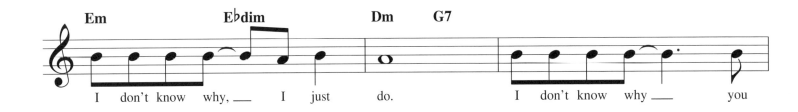

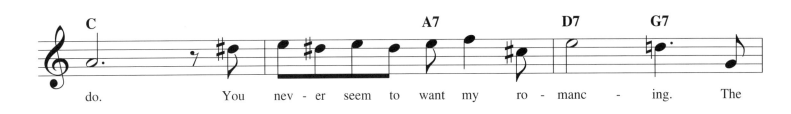

I GET ALONG WITHOUT YOU VERY WELL
(Except Sometimes)

Words and Music by HOAGY CARMICHAEL
Inspired by a poem written by J.B. THOMPSON

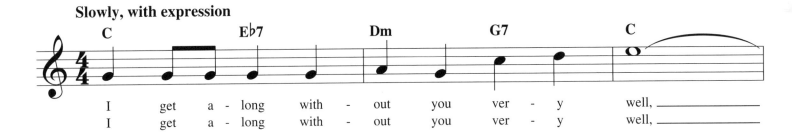
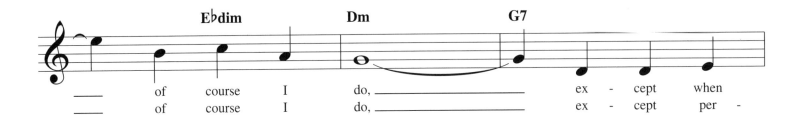
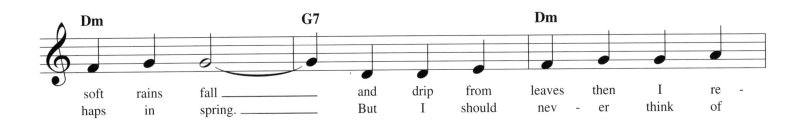
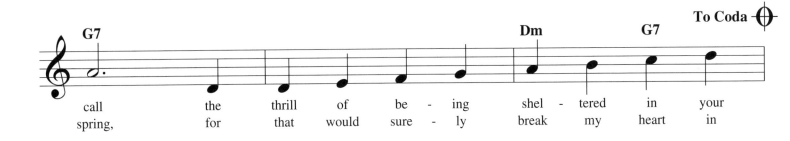
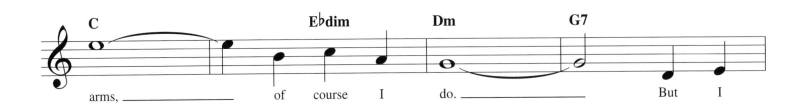

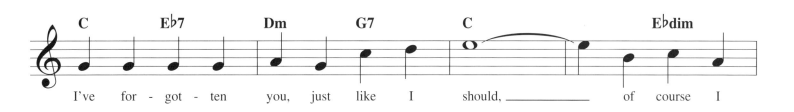
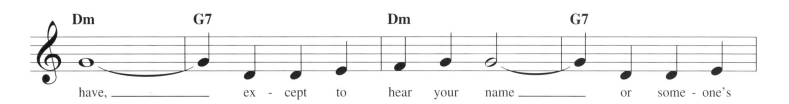
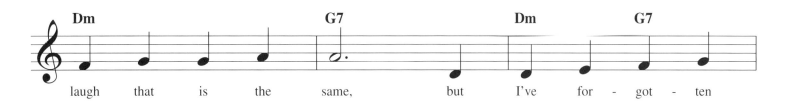
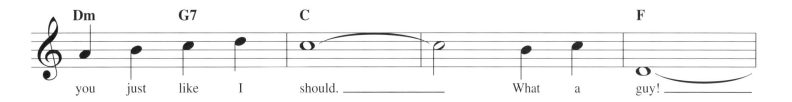

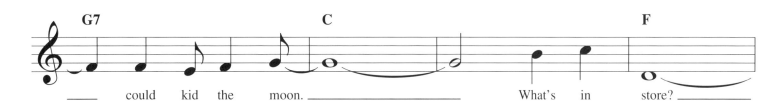

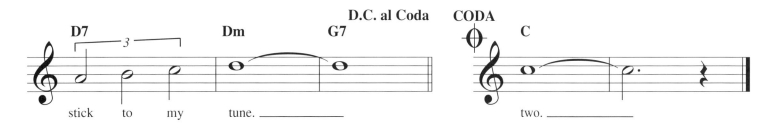

I HADN'T ANYONE TILL YOU

Copyright © 1938 by Bourne Co.
Copyright Renewed
International Copyright Secured   All Rights Reserved

Words and Music by
RAY NOBLE

Slowly, with expression

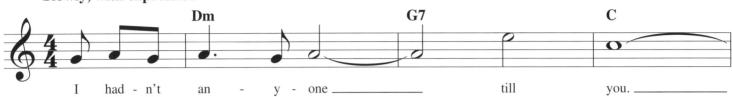

I had-n't an - y - one _____ till you. _____

_____ I was a lone - ly one _____ till you. _____

_____ I used to lie a - wake and won - der if

there could be _____ a some - one in the

wide world just made for me. Now I see. I had to

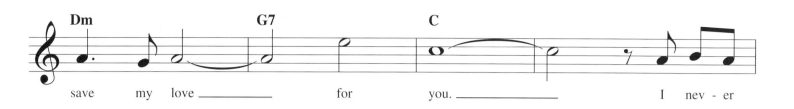

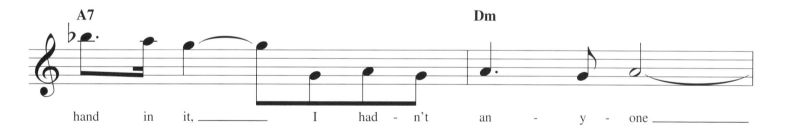
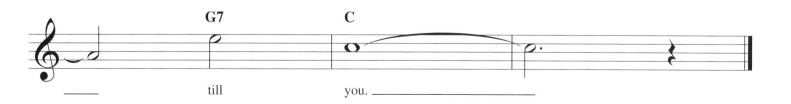

I LET A SONG GO OUT OF MY HEART

Words and Music by DUKE ELLINGTON, HENRY NEMO, JOHN REDMOND and IRVING MILLS

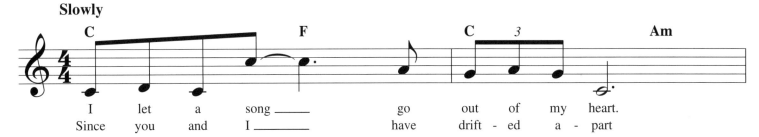

I let a song go out of my heart.
Since you and I have drift-ed a-part

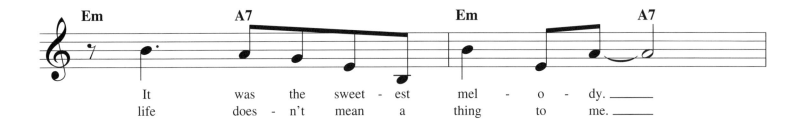

It was the sweet-est mel-o-dy.
life does-n't mean a thing to me.

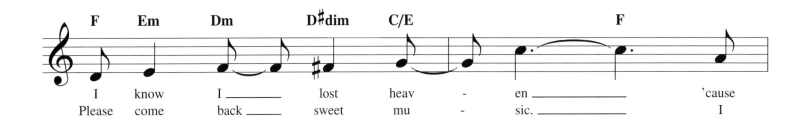

I know I lost heav-en 'cause
Please come back sweet mu-sic. I

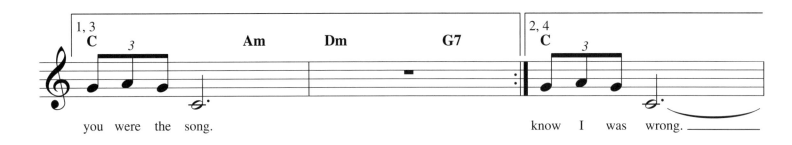

1, 3
you were the song.

2, 4
know I was wrong.

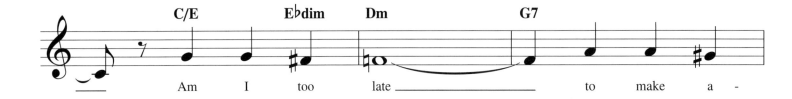

Am I too late to make a-

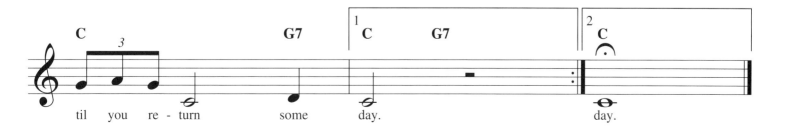

I WANNA BE LOVED

Words by BILLY ROSE and EDWARD HEYMAN
Music by JOHN GREEN

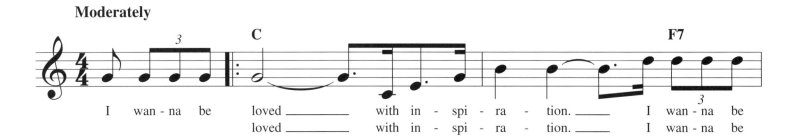
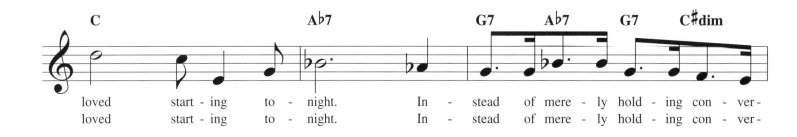

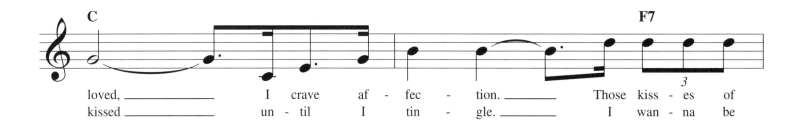
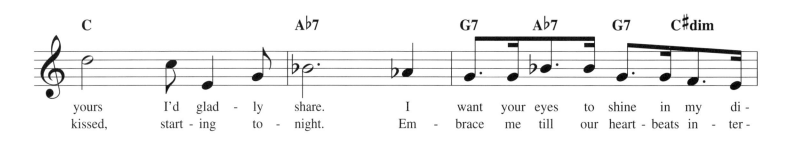
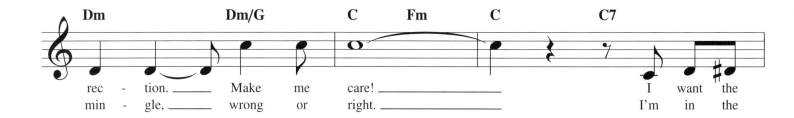

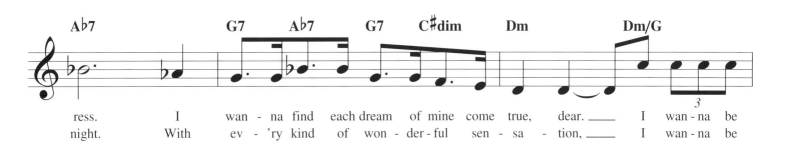

I WILL WAIT FOR YOU
from THE UMBRELLAS OF CHERBOURG

Music by MICHEL LEGRAND
Original French Text by JACQUES DEMY
English Words by NORMAN GIMBEL

Copyright © 1965 UNIVERSAL - SONGS OF POLYGRAM INTERNATIONAL, INC.,
JONWARE MUSIC CO., LES PRODUCTIONS FRANCIS LEMARQUE,
LES PRODUCTIONS MICHEL LEGRAND and NEW THUNDER MUSIC CO.
English Words Renewed by NORMAN GIMBEL and Assigned to GIMBEL MUSIC GROUP, INC.
(P.O. Box 15221, Beverly Hills, CA 90209 USA)
All Rights Reserved   Used by Permission

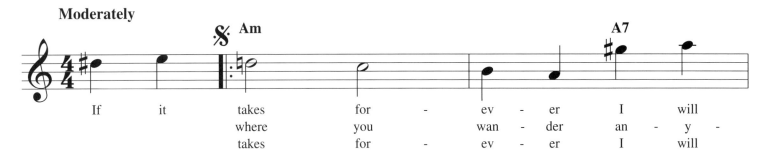

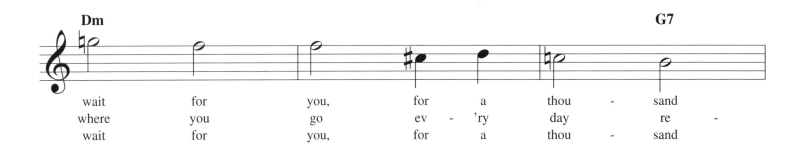

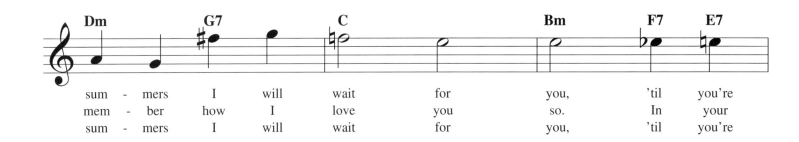

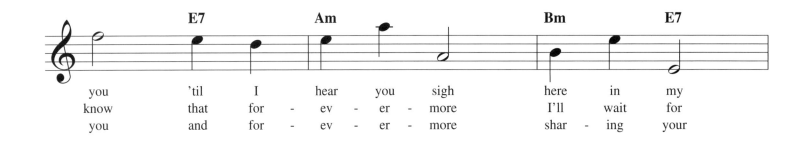

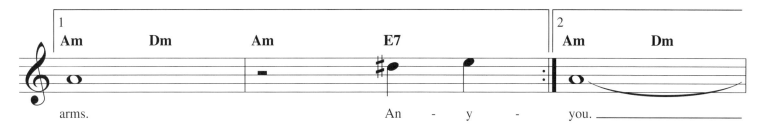
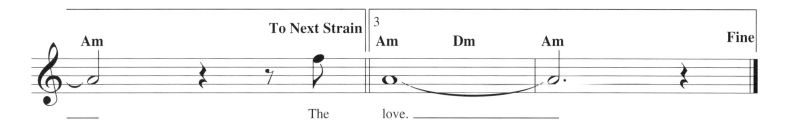
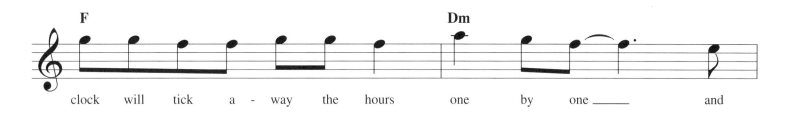

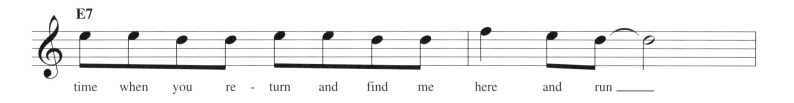
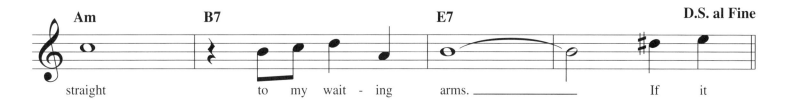

I WON'T DANCE
from ROBERTA

Words and Music by JIMMY McHUGH, DOROTHY FIELDS, JEROME KERN, OSCAR HAMMERSTEIN II and OTTO HARBACH

He: I won't dance! Don't ask me; I won't dance! Don't ask me; I won't dance, madame, with you. My heart won't let my feet do things they should do!
You know what? You're lovely. *She:* And so what? I'm lovely! *He:* But oh! what you do to me. I'm like an ocean wave that's bumped on the shore;
I won't dance! Why should I? I won't dance! How could I? I won't dance! Merci beaucoup! I know that music leads the way to romance,

I feel so absolutely stumped on the floor!

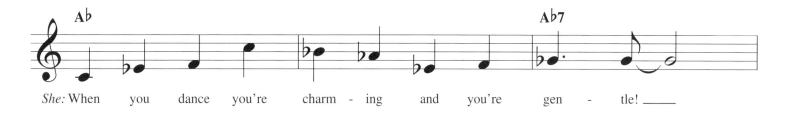

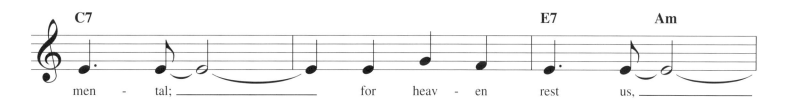
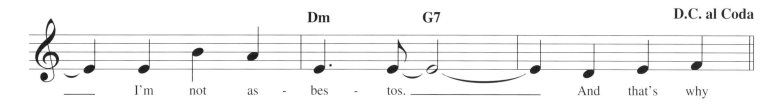
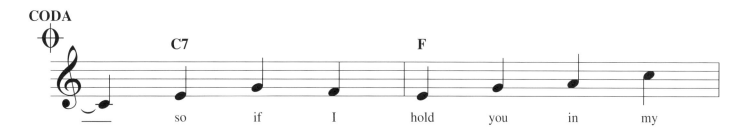

I'LL TAKE ROMANCE

Lyrics by OSCAR HAMMERSTEIN II
Music by BEN OAKLAND

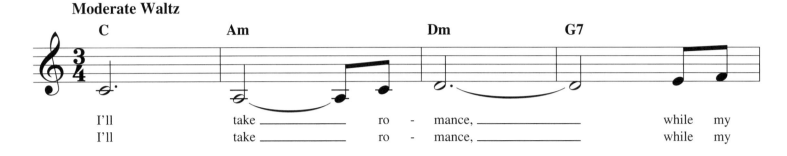
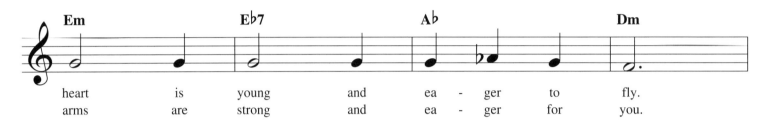
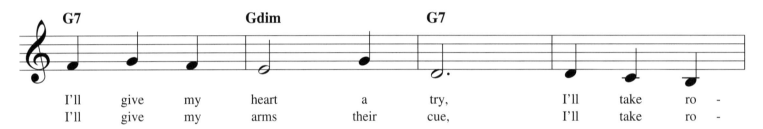
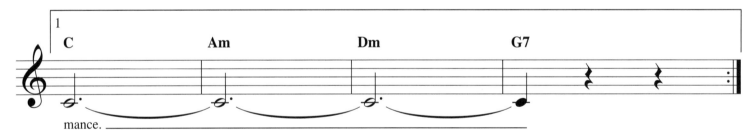
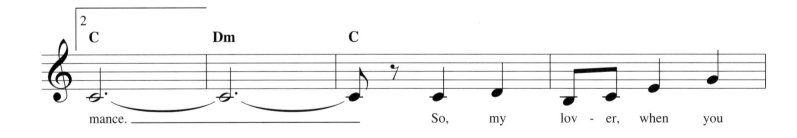
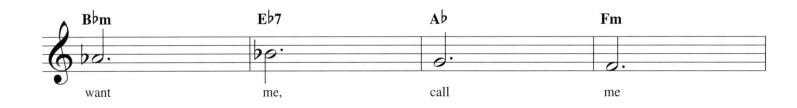

I'll take romance, while my heart is young and eager to fly.
I'll give my heart a try, I'll take romance.

I'll take romance, while my arms are strong and eager for you.
I'll give my arms their cue, I'll take romance.

So, my lover, when you want me, call me

I'm A Fool To Want You

Words and Music by JACK WOLF,
JOEL HERRON and FRANK SINATRA

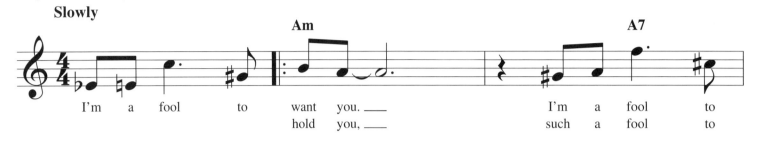
I'm a fool to want you. / I'm a fool to
hold you, / such a fool to

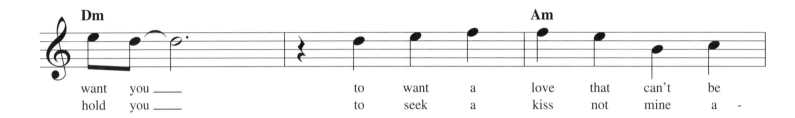
want you / to want a love that can't be
hold you / to seek a kiss not mine a-

true, a love that's there for oth-ers too. I'm a fool to
lone to share a

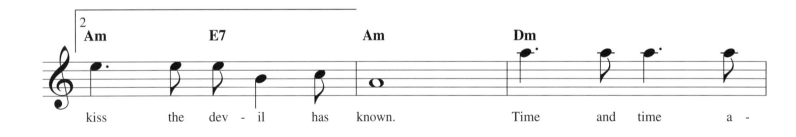
kiss the dev-il has known. Time and time a-

gain I said I'd leave you. Time and time a-

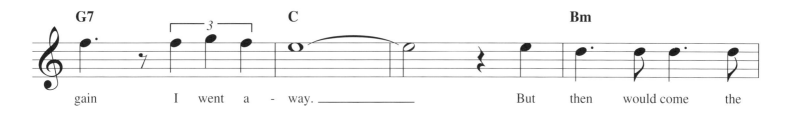

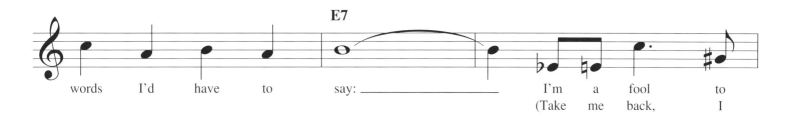
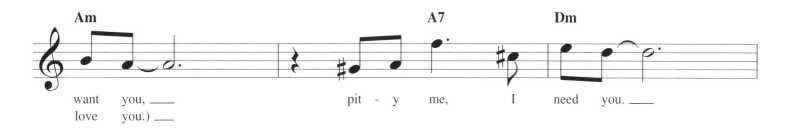

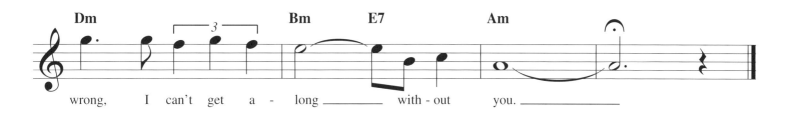

I'M CONFESSIN'
(That I Love You)

Copyright © 1930 by Bourne Co.
Copyright Renewed
International Copyright Secured   All Rights Reserved

Words and Music by AL NEIBURG,
DOC DAUGHERTY and ELLIS REYNOLDS

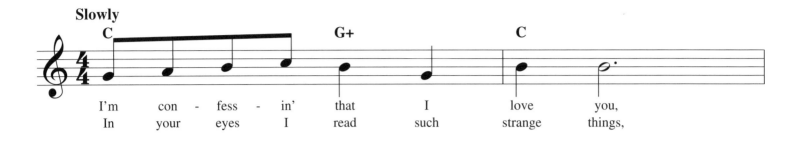

I'm con-fess-in' that I love you,
In your eyes I read such strange things,

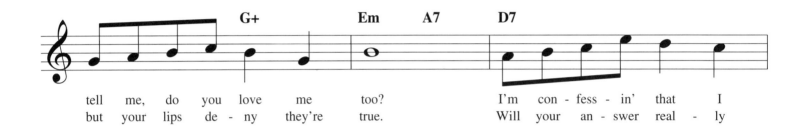

tell me, do you love me too? I'm con-fess-in' that I
but your lips de-ny they're true. Will your an-swer real-ly

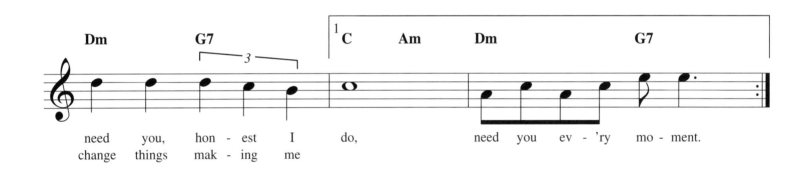

need you, hon-est I do, need you ev-'ry mo-ment.
change things mak-ing me

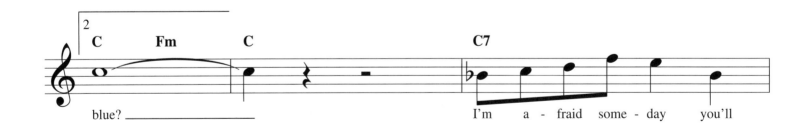

blue? I'm a-fraid some-day you'll

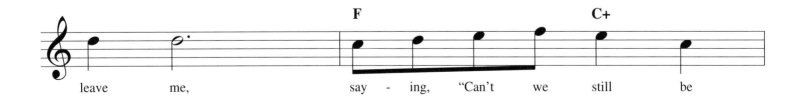

leave me, say-ing, "Can't we still be

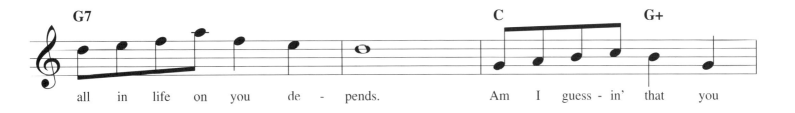

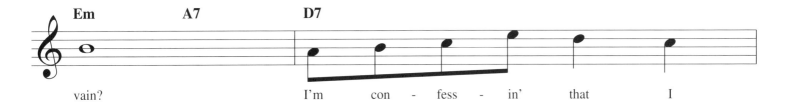
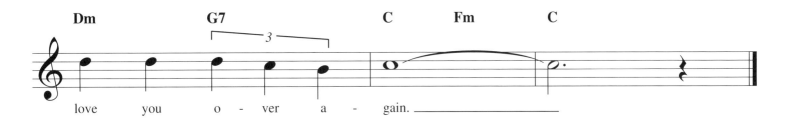

I'M OLD FASHIONED
from YOU WERE NEVER LOVELIER

Words by JOHNNY MERCER
Music by JEROME KERN

I'm old fash-ioned, I love the

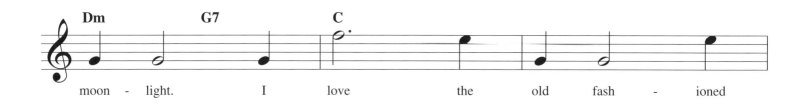
moon-light. I love the old fash-ioned

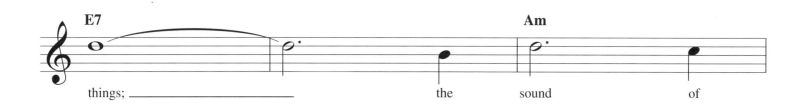
things; the sound of

rain up-on a win-dow-pane, the

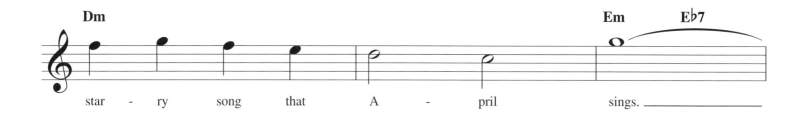
star-ry song that A-pril sings.

This year's fan-cies are

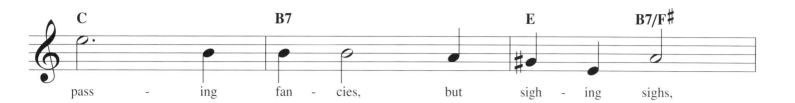

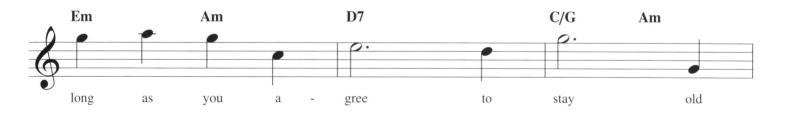
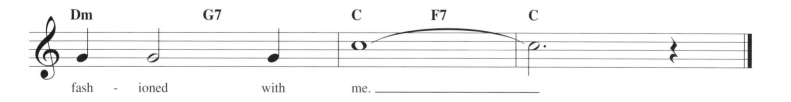

IF I SHOULD LOSE YOU
from the Paramount Picture ROSE OF THE RANCHO

Words and Music by LEO ROBIN
and RALPH RAINGER

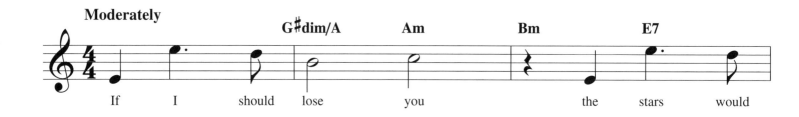
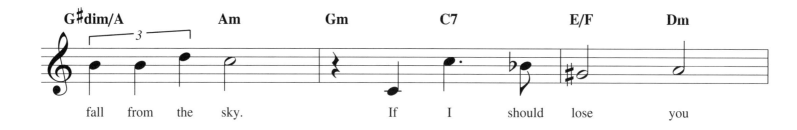
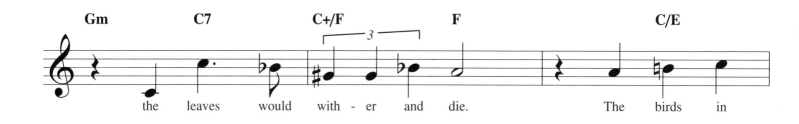

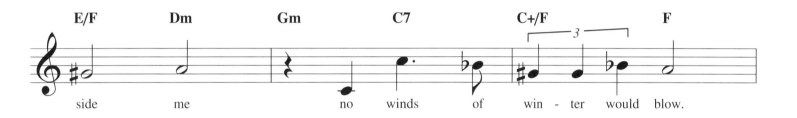

IMAGINATION

Words and Music by JOHNNY BURKE
Music by JIMMY VAN HEUSEN

Copyright © 1939, 1946 by Bourne Co., Marke Music Publishing Co., Inc.,
Limerick Music, My Dad's Songs, Inc. and Reganesque Music
Copyright Renewed
All Rights for Marke Music Publishing Co., Inc. Administered by BMG Songs
All Rights for Limerick Music, My Dad's Songs, Inc. and Reganesque Music
Administered by Spirit Two Music, Inc.
International Copyright Secured   All Rights Reserved

I-mag-i-na-tion is fun-ny. It

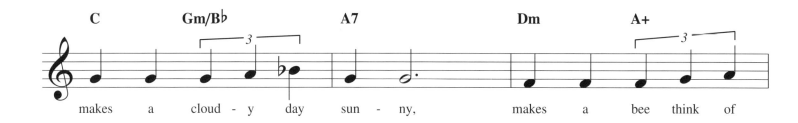

makes a cloud-y day sun-ny, makes a bee think of

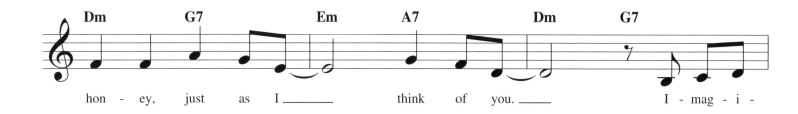

hon-ey, just as I _____ think of you. _____ I-mag-i-

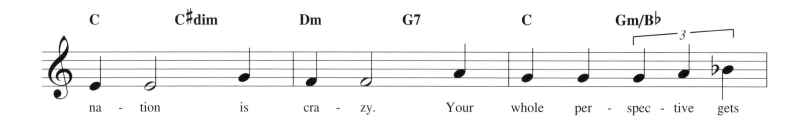

na-tion is cra-zy. Your whole per-spec-tive gets

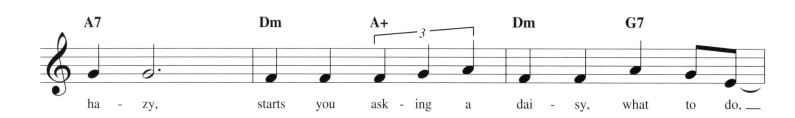

ha-zy, starts you ask-ing a dai-sy, what to do, _____

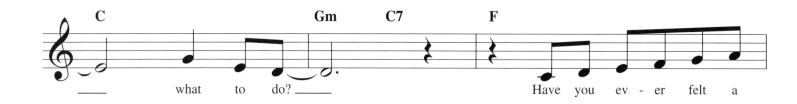

_____ what to do? _____ Have you ev-er felt a

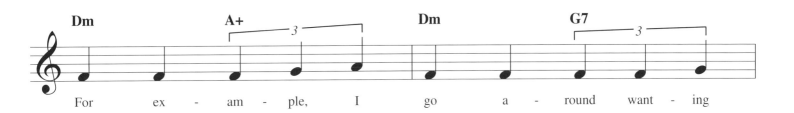

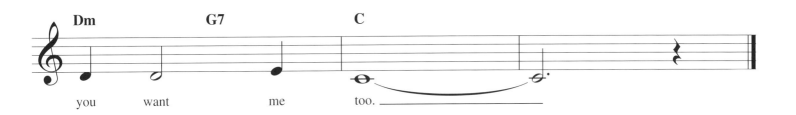

IN LOVE IN VAIN

Words by LEO ROBIN
Music by JEROME KERN

Copyright © 1946 Leo Robin Music Company
and Universal - PolyGram International Publishing, Inc.
Copyright Renewed
All Rights for Leo Robin Music Company Administered by Music Sales Corporation (ASCAP)
International Copyright Secured All Rights Reserved
Reprinted by Permission

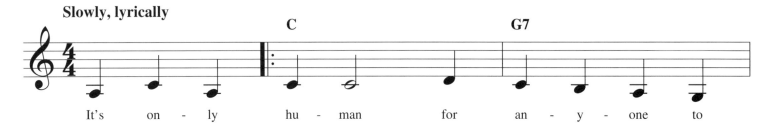

It's on-ly hu-man for an-y-one to

want to be in love, but who wants to

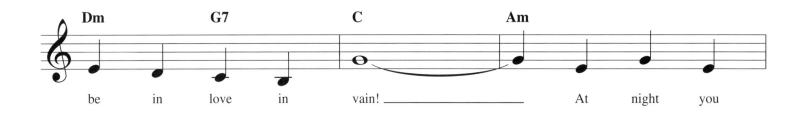

be in love in vain! At night you

hang a-round the house and eat your heart out,

and cry your eyes out and wrack your

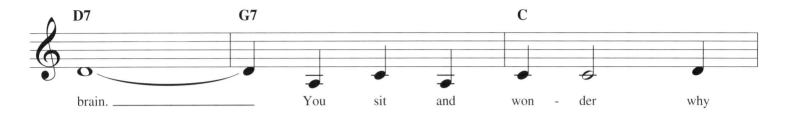
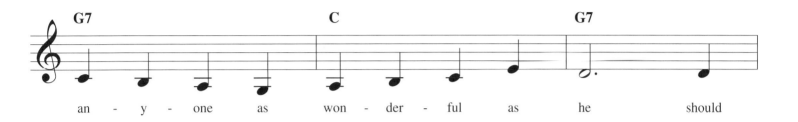
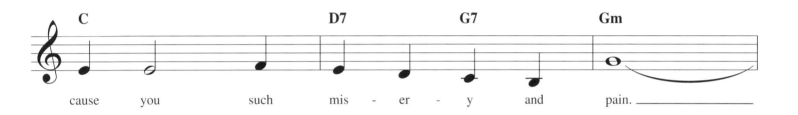
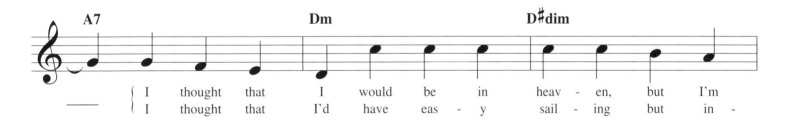

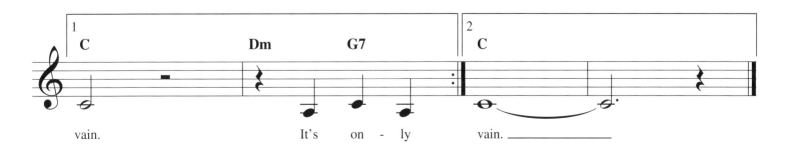

Is You Is, Or Is You Ain't
(Ma' Baby)
from FOLLOW THE BOYS
from FIVE GUYS NAMED MOE

Copyright © 1943, 1944 UNIVERSAL MUSIC CORP.
Copyright Renewed
All Rights Reserved   Used by Permission

Words and Music by BILLY AUSTIN
and LOUIS JORDAN

Jazz Blues

Is you is, or is you ain't, ma' ba-by?

The way you're act-ing late-ly makes me doubt.

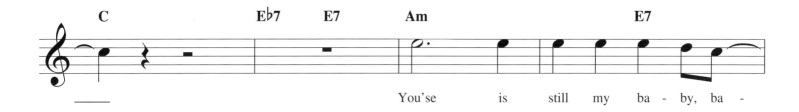
You'se is still my ba-by, ba-

-by.   Seems my flame in your heart's done gone out.

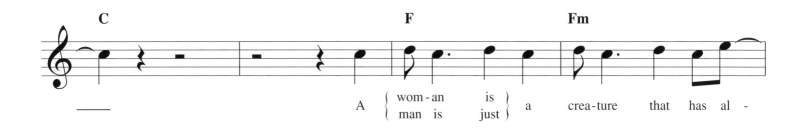
A { wom-an is / man is just } a crea-ture that has al-

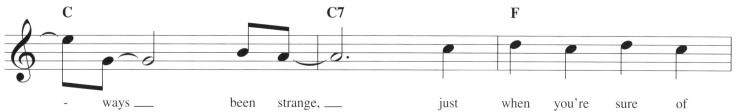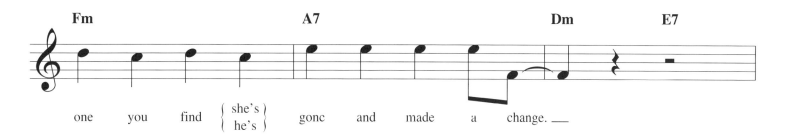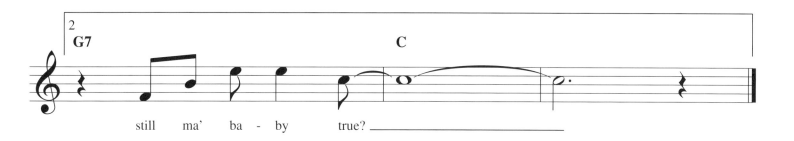

IT DON'T MEAN A THING
(If It Ain't Got That Swing)
from SOPHISTICATED LADIES
featured in the Broadway Musical SWING!

Copyright © 1932 (Renewed 1959) and Assigned to Famous Music LLC
and EMI Mills Music Inc. in the U.S.A.
Rights for the world outside the U.S.A. Controlled by EMI Mills Music Inc. (Publishing)
and Alfred Publishing Co., (Print)
International Copyright Secured   All Rights Reserved

Words and Music by DUKE ELLINGTON
and IRVING MILLS

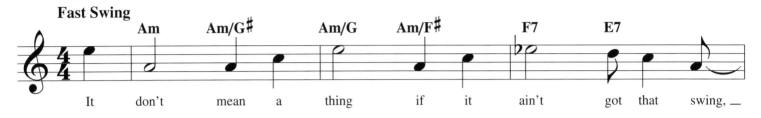

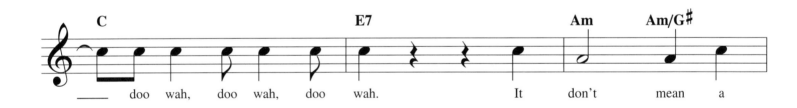

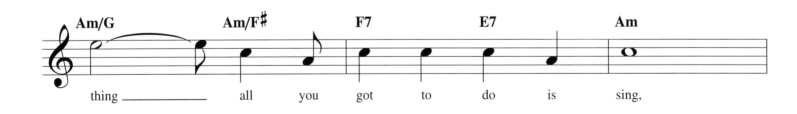

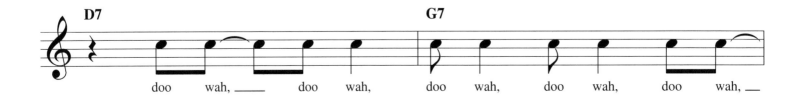

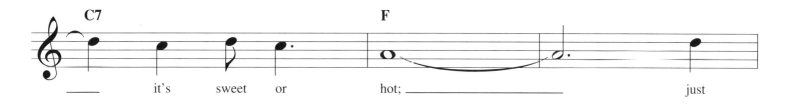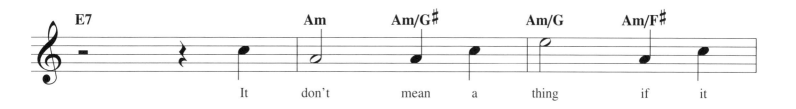

IT'S A BLUE WORLD

Words and Music by BOB WRIGHT and CHET FORREST

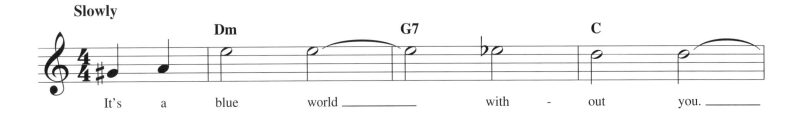
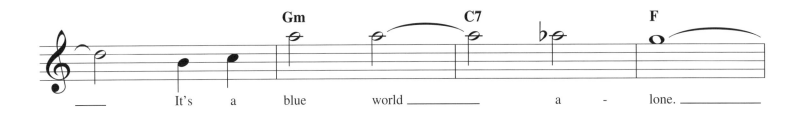

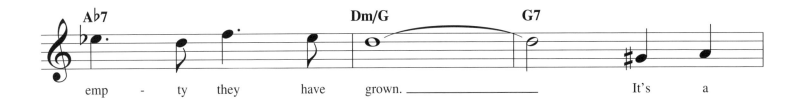

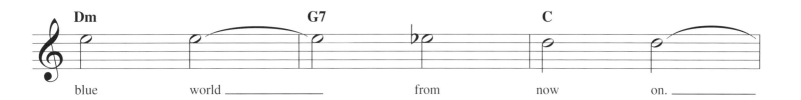
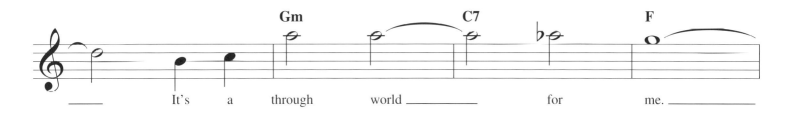

IT'S EASY TO REMEMBER
from the Paramount Picture MISSISSIPPI

Words by LORENZ HART
Music by RICHARD RODGERS

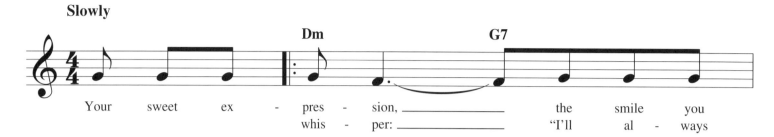

Your sweet ex - pres - sion, the smile you
whis - per: "I'll al - ways

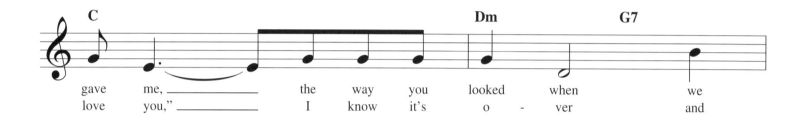

gave me, the way you looked when we
love you," I know it's o - ver and

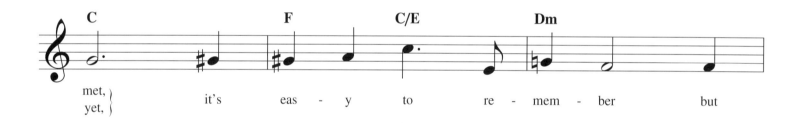

met, } it's eas - y to re - mem - ber but
yet,

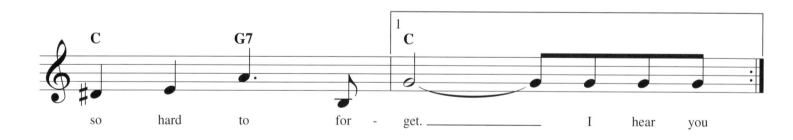

so hard to for - get. I hear you

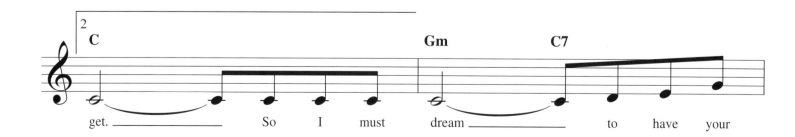

get. So I must dream to have your

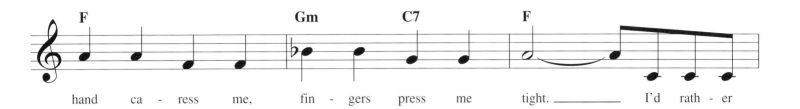
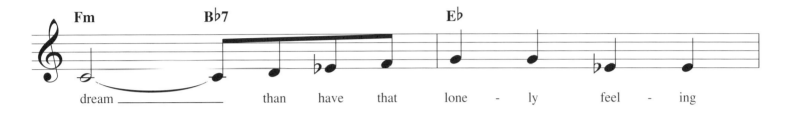
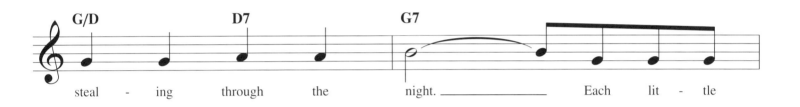

JUST ONE MORE CHANCE

Words by SAM COSLOW
Music by ARTHUR JOHNSTON

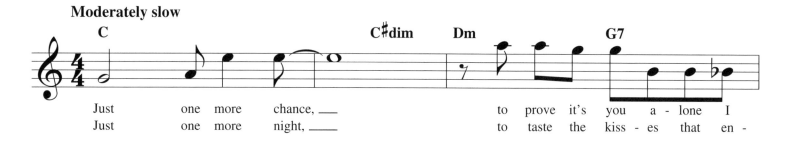

Just one more chance, ___ to prove it's you a - lone I
Just one more night, ___ to taste the kiss - es that en -

care for, each night I say a lit - tle prayer for
chant me, I'd want no oth - ers if you'd grant me

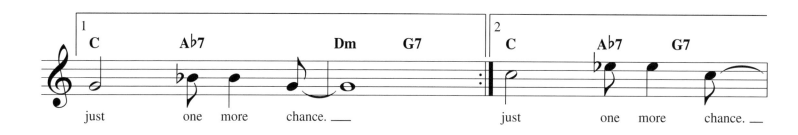

1. just one more chance. ___
2. just one more chance. ___

I've learned the mean - ing of re -

pen - tance. Now you're the ju - ry at my trial.

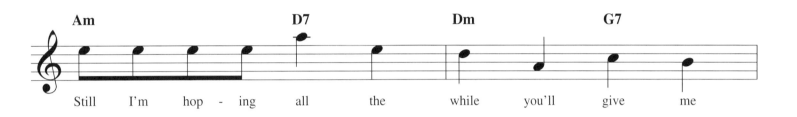
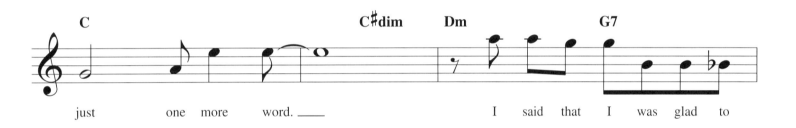
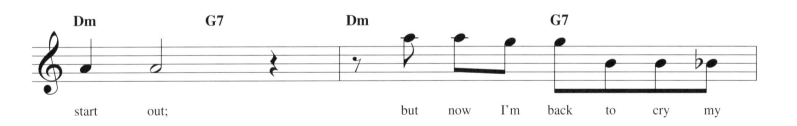

THE LADY IS A TRAMP
from BABES IN ARMS
from WORDS AND MUSIC

Words by LORENZ HART
Music by RICHARD RODGERS

I get too hungry for dinner at eight,
I don't like crap games with barons and earls.

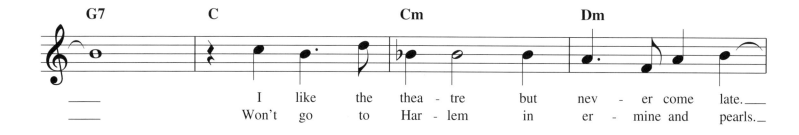

I like the theatre but never come late.
Won't go to Harlem in ermine and pearls.

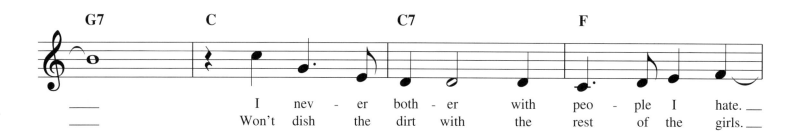

I never bother with people I hate.
Won't dish the dirt with the rest of the girls.

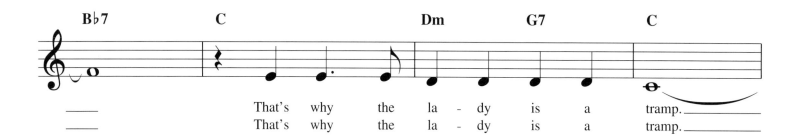

That's why the lady is a tramp.
That's why the lady is a tramp.

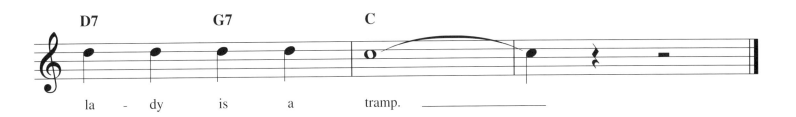

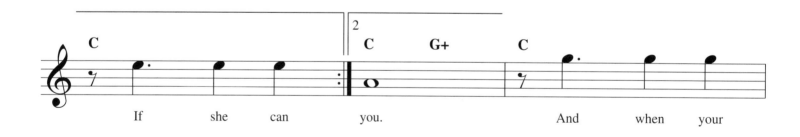
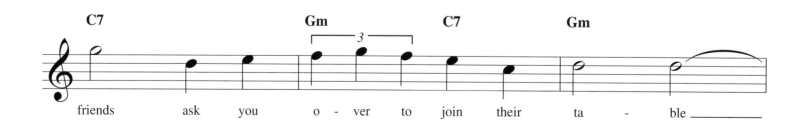

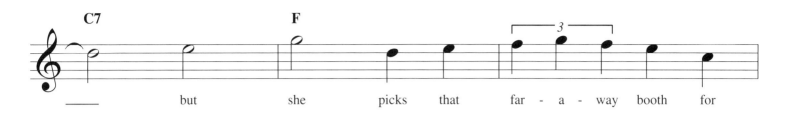

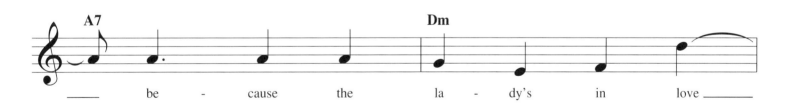

LEARNIN' THE BLUES

Words and Music by
DOLORES "VICKI" SILVERS

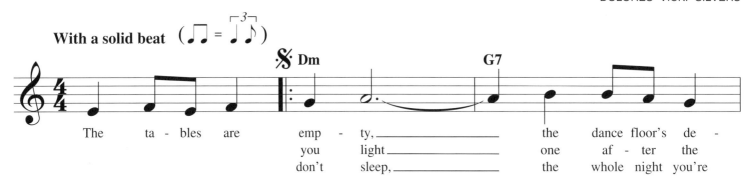

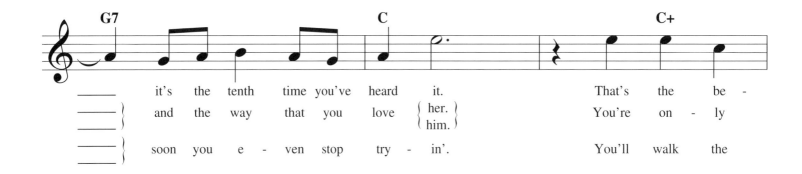
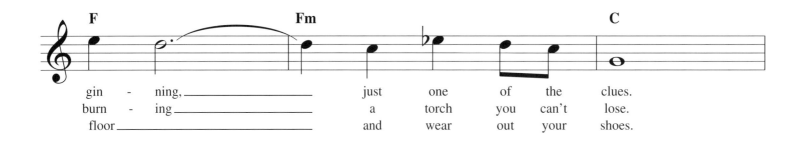
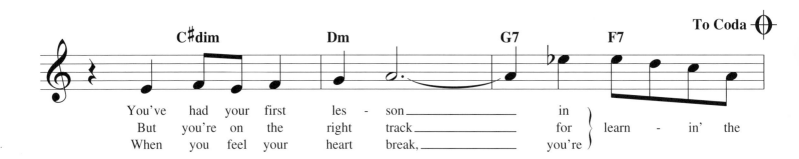

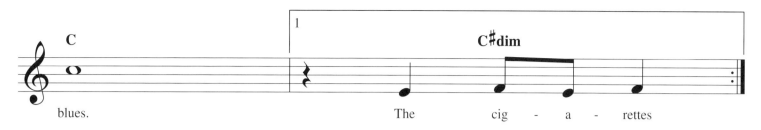
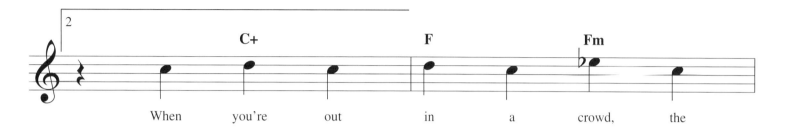
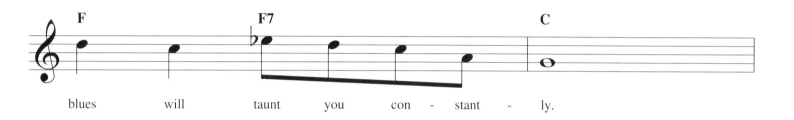
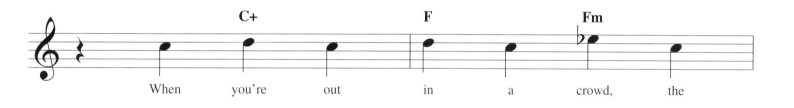
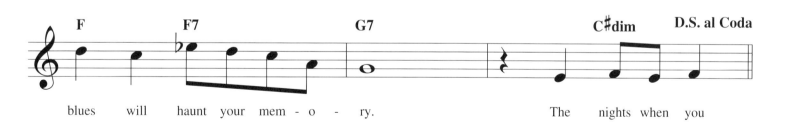

LET THERE BE YOU

Words and Music by VICKI YOUNG and DAVID CAVANAUGH

Let there be light, and there was a light.

Let there be earth, and there was earth. If

I had my way, I would ask of Him, please let there be

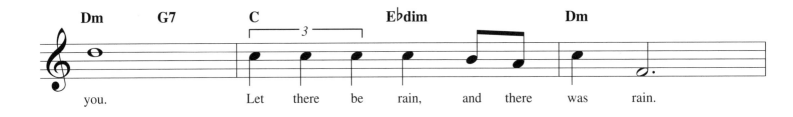
you. Let there be rain, and there was rain.

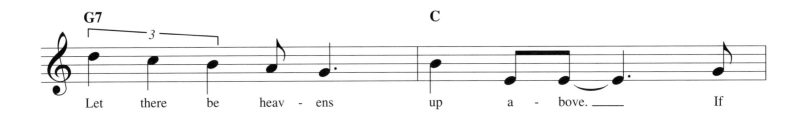
Let there be heav-ens up a-bove. If

I had my way, I would ask of Him, please let there be

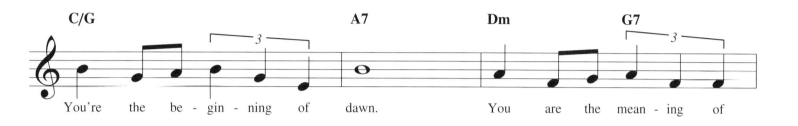

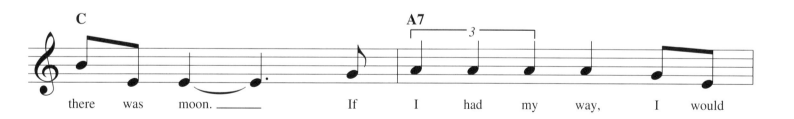
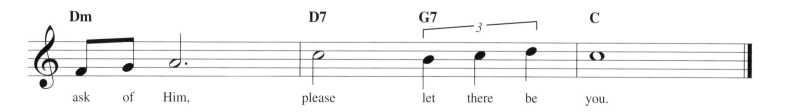

LET'S FALL IN LOVE

Words by TED KOEHLER
Music by HAROLD ARLEN

LIKE SOMEONE IN LOVE

Words by JOHNNY BURKE
Music by JIMMY VAN HEUSEN

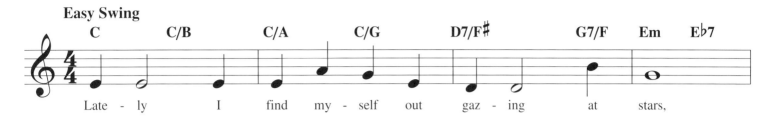

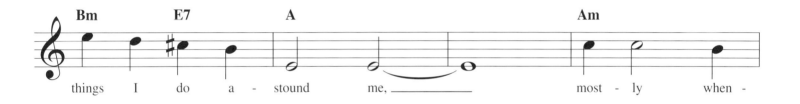
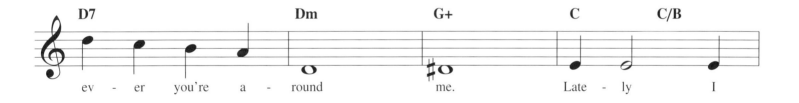

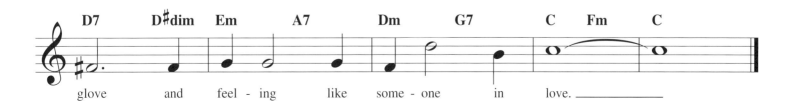

LITTLE GIRL BLUE
from JUMBO

Words by LORENZ HART
Music by RICHARD RODGERS

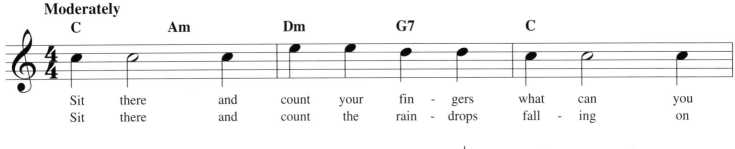
Sit there and count your fin-gers what can you do?
Sit there and count the rain-drops fall-ing on you.

Old girl you're through. Sit there and
It's time you knew, all you can

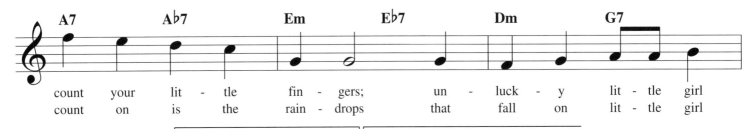
count your lit-tle fin-gers; un-luck-y lit-tle girl
count on is the rain-drops that fall on lit-tle girl

blue.
blue. No use, old girl, you

may as well sur-ren-der; your hope is get-ting

slen-der. Why won't some-bod-y send a ten-der

blue boy to cheer a lit-tle girl blue?

A Lovely Way To Spend An Evening

LOVE YOU MADLY

By DUKE ELLINGTON

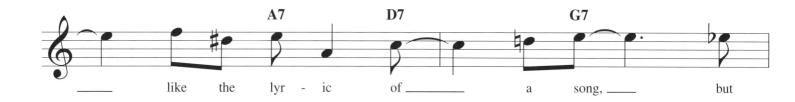

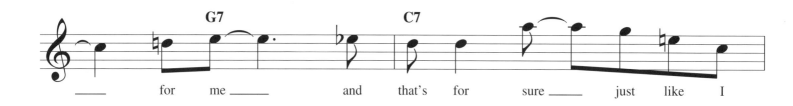

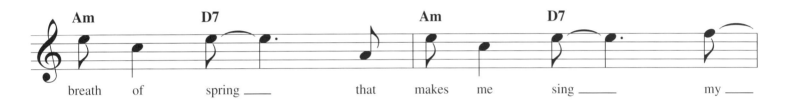

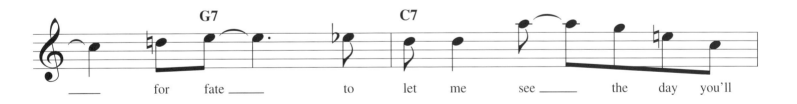

Lullaby of the Leaves

Words by JOE YOUNG
Music by BERNICE PETKERE

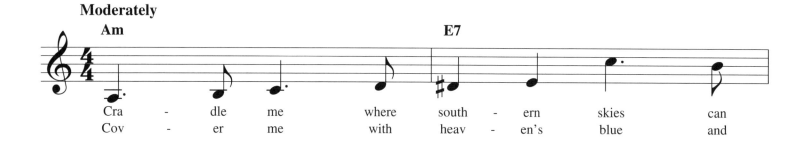
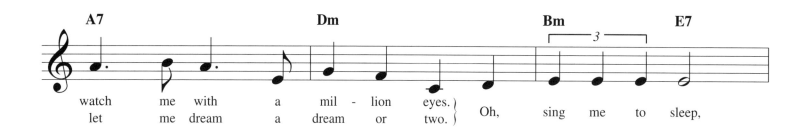
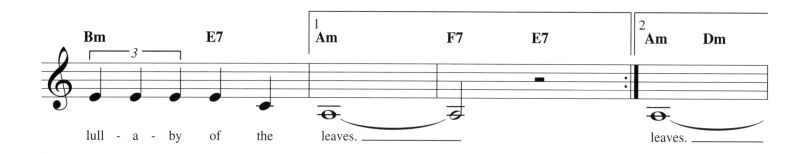
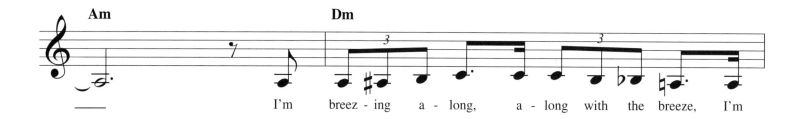

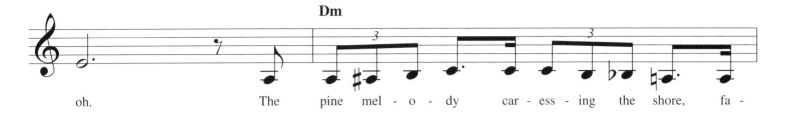

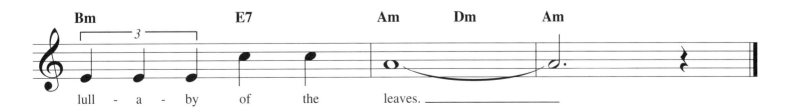

MEDITATION
(Meditacāo)

Music by ANTONIO CARLOS JOBIM
Original Words by NEWTON MENDONÇA
English Words by NORMAN GIMBEL

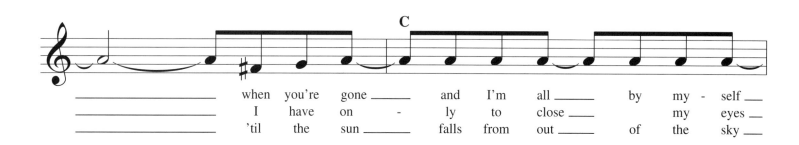
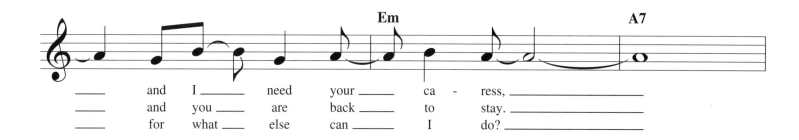

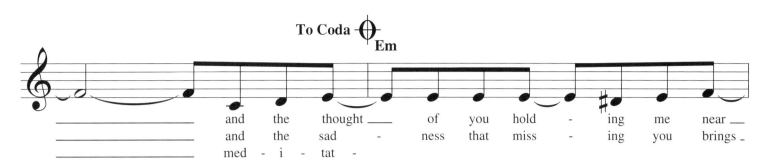

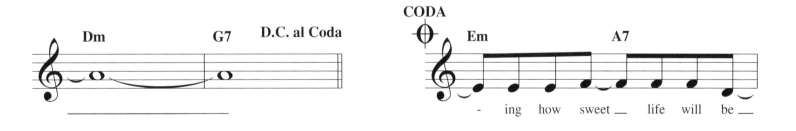
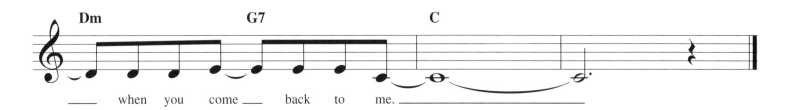

More Than You Know

Words by WILLIAM ROSE and EDWARD ELISCU
Music by VINCENT YOUMANS

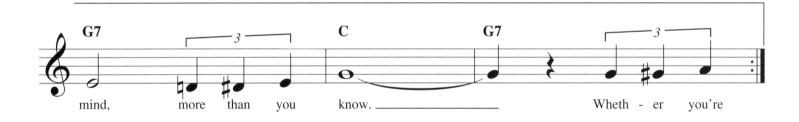

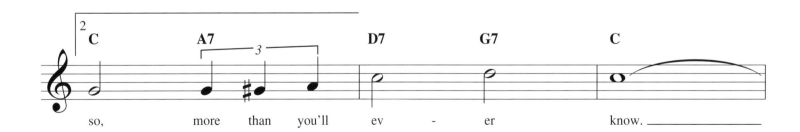

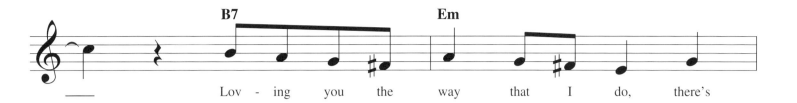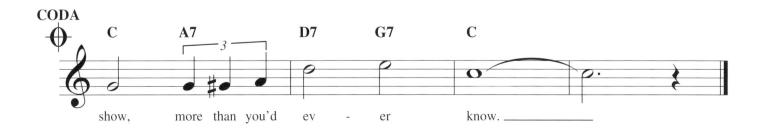

MY IDEAL
from the Paramount Picture PLAYBOY OF PARIS

Words by LEO ROBIN
Music by RICHARD A. WHITING and NEWELL CHASE

Copyright © 1930 (Renewed 1957) by Famous Music LLC
International Copyright Secured   All Rights Reserved

Will I ever find the {girl/boy} in my mind, the one who is my i-

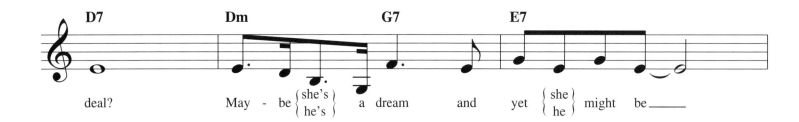
deal? May-be {she's/he's} a dream and yet {she/he} might be

just a-round the cor-ner wait-ing for me.

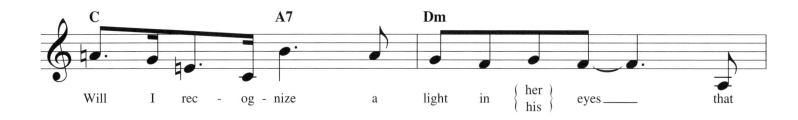
Will I rec-og-nize a light in {her/his} eyes that

no oth-er eyes re-veal, or will I pass {her/him} by and
al-tho' {she/he} may be late, I
nev-er e-ven know that {she/he} is my i-deal.
trust in fate and so I wait for my i-deal.

My Lucky Star

Words and Music by B.G. DeSYLVA, LEW BROWN and RAY HENDERSON

Copyright © 1928 by Chappell & Co., Stephen Ballentine Music Publishing Co. and Ray Henderson Music
Copyright Renewed
International Copyright Secured All Rights Reserved

Moderately

I'd like to find my luck-y star, _____ its ti-ny light has

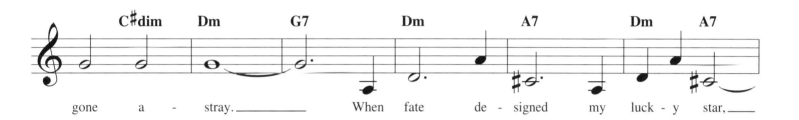
gone a - stray. _____ When fate de - signed my luck-y star, _____

_____ there must have been a hol - i - day. _____ Why can't I

be as oth - ers are _____ whose lives are like the month of

May? _____ Be good to me, my luck - y star, _____

_____ and send the one I love my way! _____

MY OLD FLAME
from the Paramount Picture BELLE OF THE NINETIES

Copyright © 1934 (Renewed 1961) by Famous Music LLC
International Copyright Secured   All Rights Reserved

Words and Music by ARTHUR JOHNSTON
and SAM COSLOW

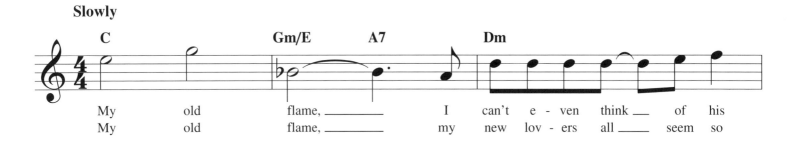

My old flame, I can't even think of his
My old flame, my new lovers all seem so

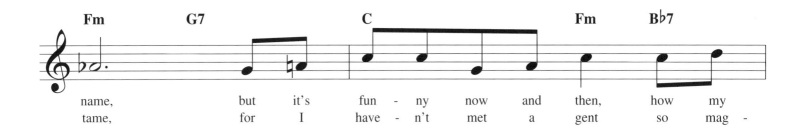

name, but it's funny now and then, how my
tame, for I haven't met a gent so mag-

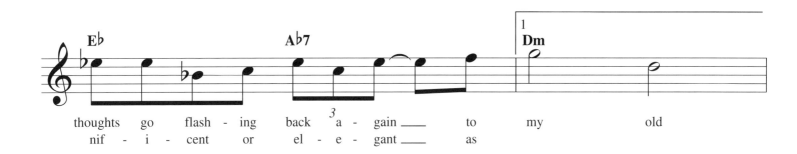

thoughts go flashing back again to my old
nif-i-cent or el-e-gant as

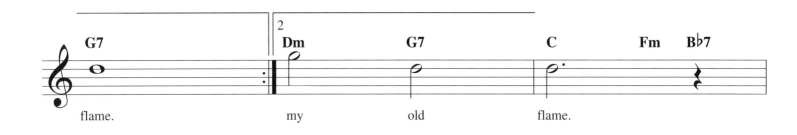

flame. my old flame.

I've met so many who had fas-ci-natin' ways, a

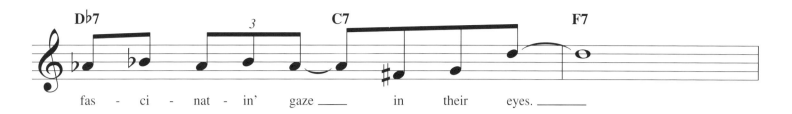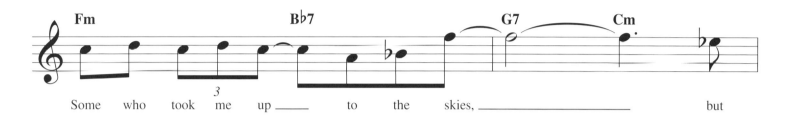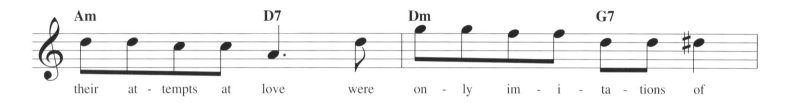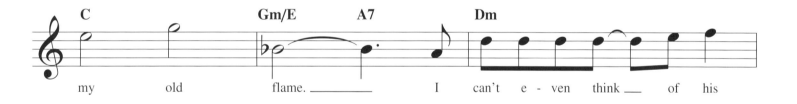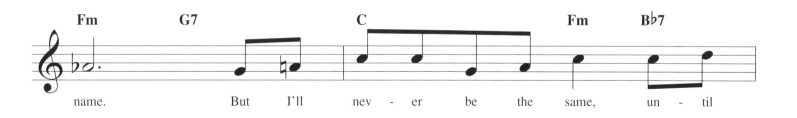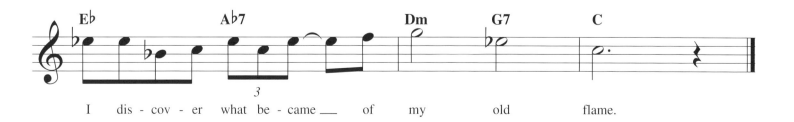

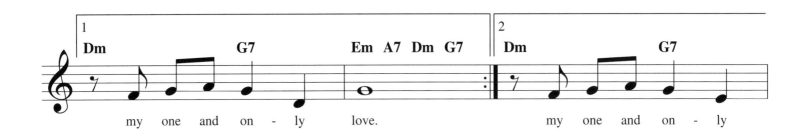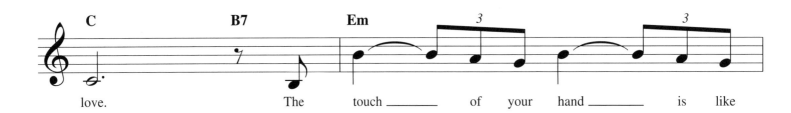

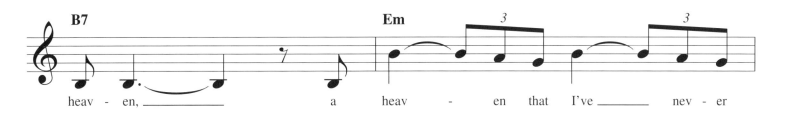
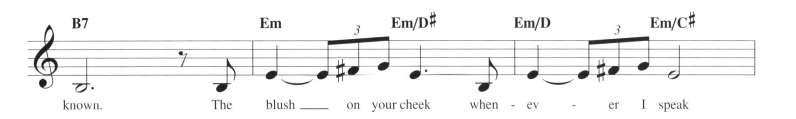
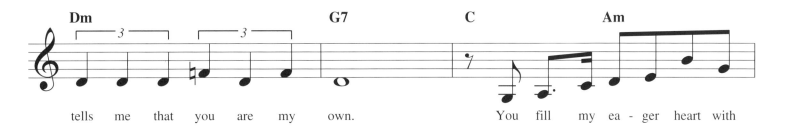

MY SHINING HOUR
from the Motion Picture THE SKY'S THE LIMIT

Lyrics by JOHNNY MERCER
Music by HAROLD ARLEN

© 1943 (Renewed) HARWIN MUSIC CO.
All Rights Reserved

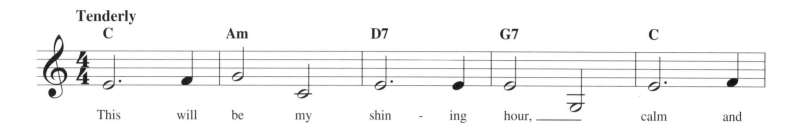

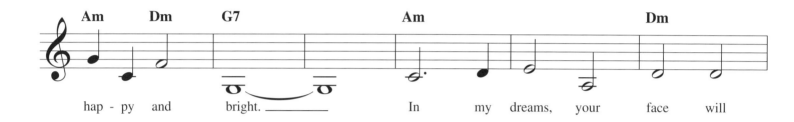

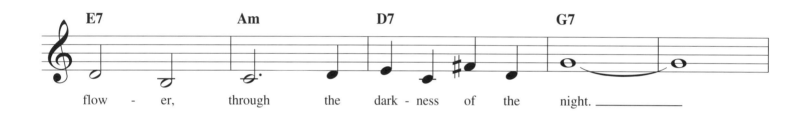

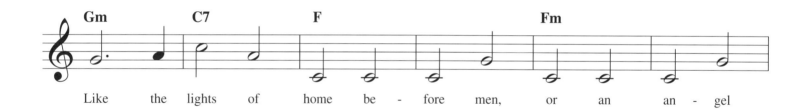

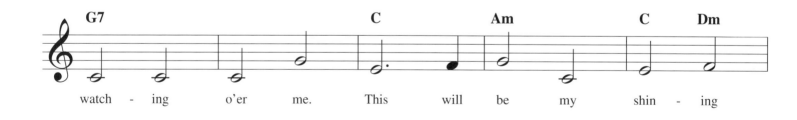

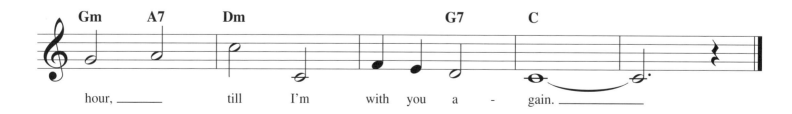

SOME DAY MY PRINCE WILL COME

Words by LARRY MOREY
Music by FRANK CHURCHILL

Copyright © 1937 by Bourne Co.
Copyright Renewed
International Copyright Secured   All Rights Reserved

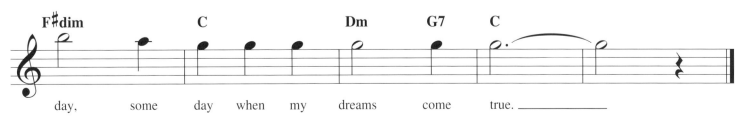

NANCY – WITH THE LAUGHING FACE

Words by PHIL SILVERS
Music by JAMES VAN HEUSEN

Slowly, with expression

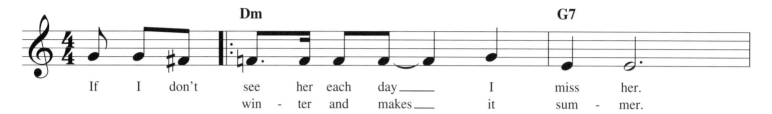

If I don't see her each day___ I miss her.
win - ter and makes___ it sum - mer.

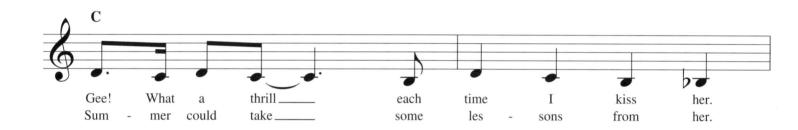

Gee! What a thrill___ each time I kiss her.
Sum - mer could take___ some les - sons from her.

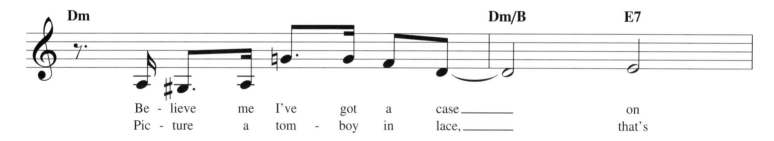

Be - lieve me I've got a case___ on
Pic - ture a tom - boy in lace,___ that's

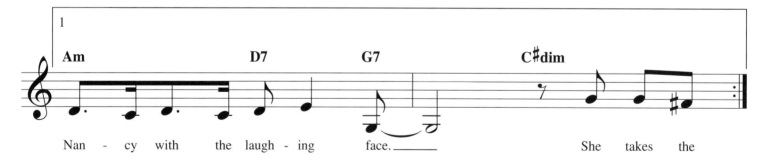

1.
Nan - cy with the laugh - ing face.___ She takes the

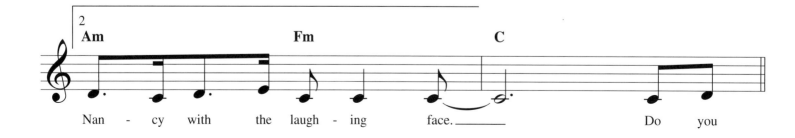

2.
Nan - cy with the laugh - ing face.___ Do you

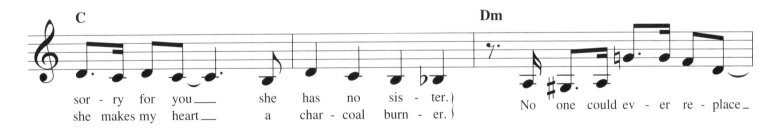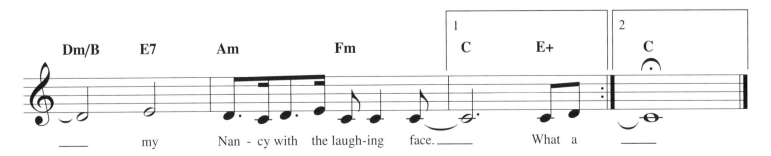

THE NEARNESS OF YOU
from the Paramount Picture ROMANCE IN THE DARK

Words by NED WASHINGTON
Music by HOAGY CARMICHAEL

Slow and bluesy

It's not the pale moon that excites me, that thrills and delights me. Oh,

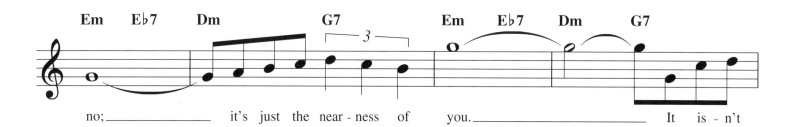

no; it's just the nearness of you. It isn't

your sweet conversation that brings this sensation. Oh,

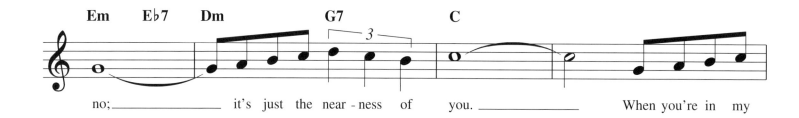

no; it's just the nearness of you. When you're in my

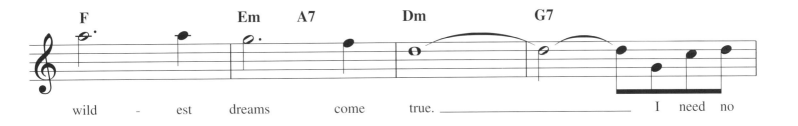

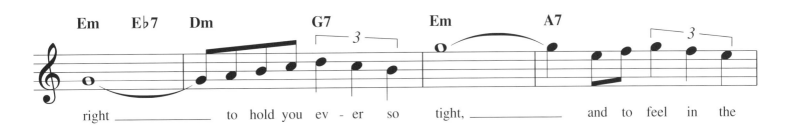
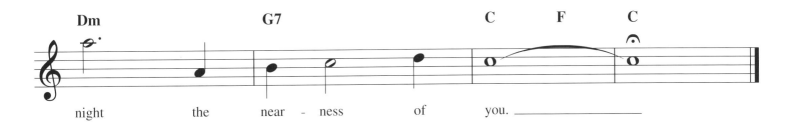

NEVER LET ME GO
from the Paramount Picture THE SCARLET HOUR

Copyright © 1956 (Renewed 1984) by Famous Music LLC
International Copyright Secured   All Rights Reserved

Words and Music by JAY LIVINGSTON
and RAY EVANS

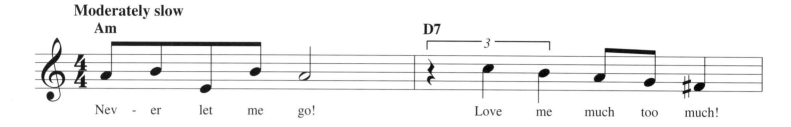
Nev-er let me go! Love me much too much!

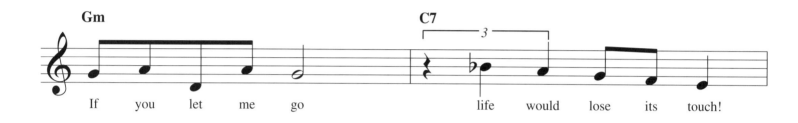
If you let me go life would lose its touch!

What would I be with-out you? There's no place for me with-

out you! Nev-er let me go! I'd be so lost if

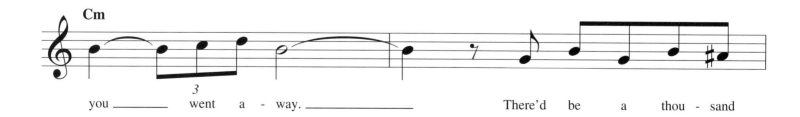
you went a-way. There'd be a thou-sand

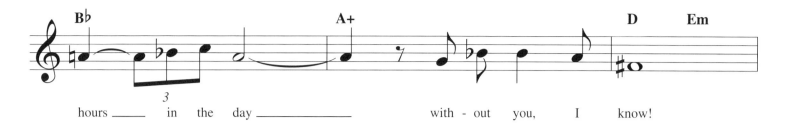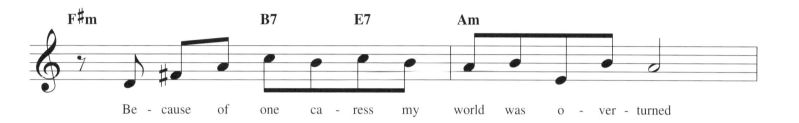

A NIGHTINGALE SANG IN BERKELEY SQUARE

Lyric by ERIC MASCHWITZ
Music by MANNING SHERWIN

Copyright © 1940 The Peter Maurice Music Co., Ltd., London, England
Copyright Renewed and Assigned to Shapiro, Bernstein & Co., Inc., New York for U.S.A. and Canada
International Copyright Secured All Rights Reserved
Used by Permission

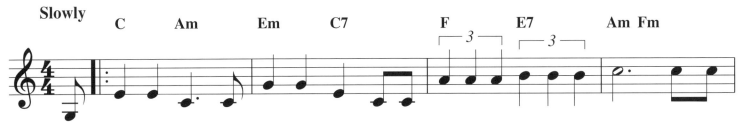

That cer-tain night, the night we met, there was mag-ic a-broad in the air. There were
strange it was, how sweet and strange, there was nev-er a dream to com-pare. With that

an-gels din-ing at the Ritz, and a { night-in-gale sang in Berk-'ley
ha-zy, cra-zy night we met, when a {

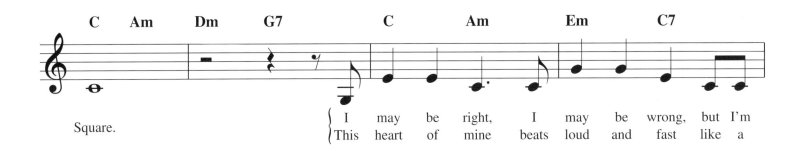

Square. { I may be right, I may be wrong, but I'm
This heart of mine beats loud and fast like a

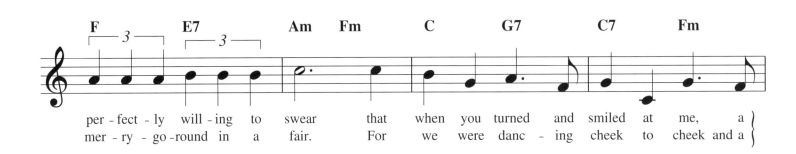

per-fect-ly will-ing to swear that when you turned and smiled at me, a
mer-ry-go-round in a fair. For we were danc-ing cheek to cheek and a

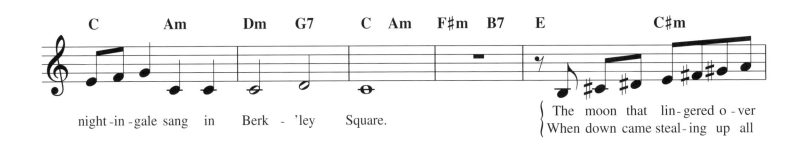

night-in-gale sang in Berk-'ley Square. { The moon that lin-gered o-ver
When down came steal-ing up all

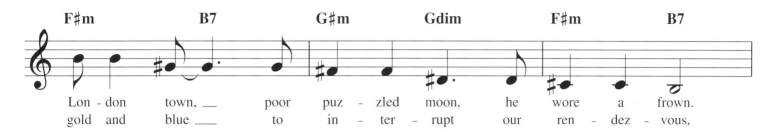

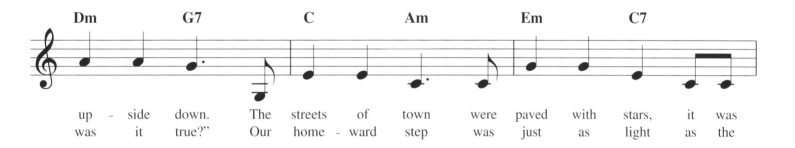

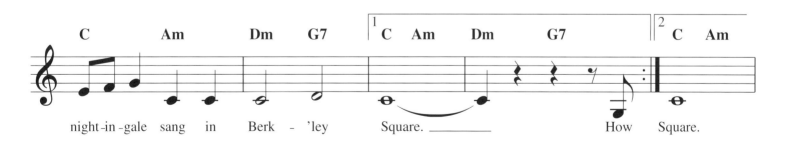

ONE FOR MY BABY
(And One More for the Road)
from the Motion Picture THE SKY'S THE LIMIT

© 1943 (Renewed) HARWIN MUSIC CO.
All Rights Reserved

Lyric by JOHNNY MERCER
Music by HAROLD ARLEN

Lazily

It's quar - ter to three, ___ there's no one in the place ex -
got the rou - tine, ___ so drop an - oth - er nick - el
that's how it goes, ___ and Joe, I know you're get - ting

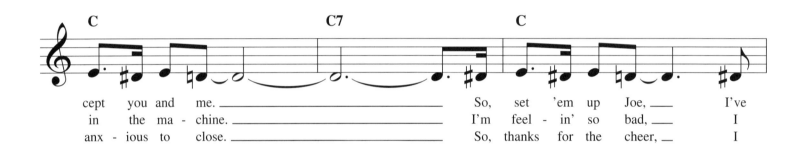

cept you and me. ___ So, set 'em up Joe, ___ I've
in the ma - chine. ___ I'm feel - in' so bad, ___ I
anx - ious to close. ___ So, thanks for the cheer, ___ I

got a lit - tle sto - ry you ought - a know. ___ We're
wish you'd make the mu - sic dream - y and sad. ___ Could
hope you did - n't mind my bend - ing your ear. ___ This

drink - ing, my friend, ___ to the end ___ of a brief ep - i - sode. ___
tell you a lot, ___ but you've got ___ to be true to your code. ___
torch that I've found ___ must be drowned ___ or it might ex - plode. ___

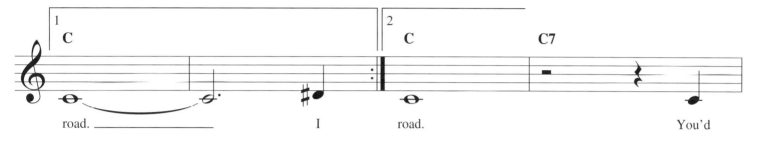

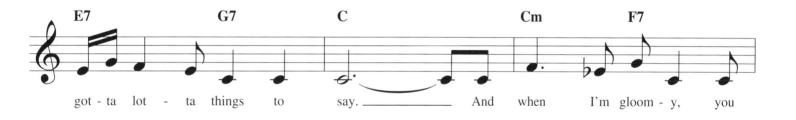
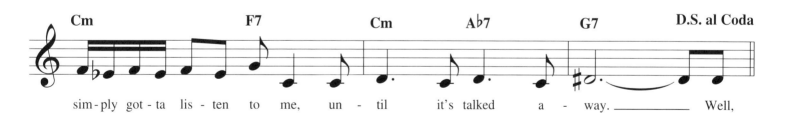
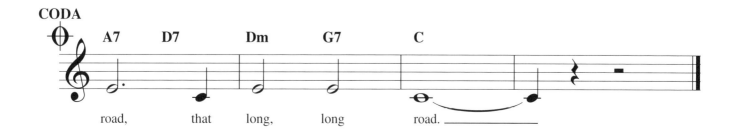

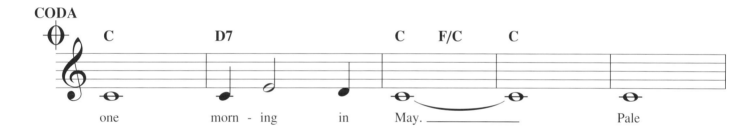
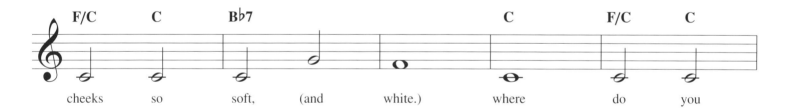
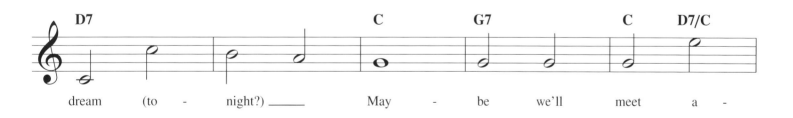
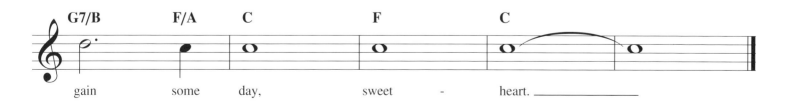

ONE NOTE SAMBA
(Samba De Una Nota So)

Original Lyrics by NEWTON MENDONÇA
English Lyrics by ANTONIO CARLOS JOBIM
Music by ANTONIO CARLOS JOBIM

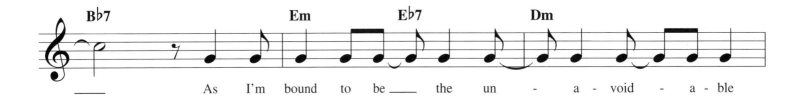

ONLY TRUST YOUR HEART

Words by SAMMY CAHN
Music by BENNY CARTER

Copyright © 1964 UNIVERSAL MUSIC CORP.
Copyright Renewed
All Rights Reserved   Used by Permission

Moderate Latin

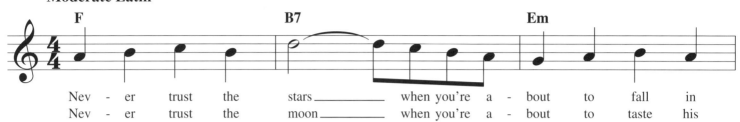

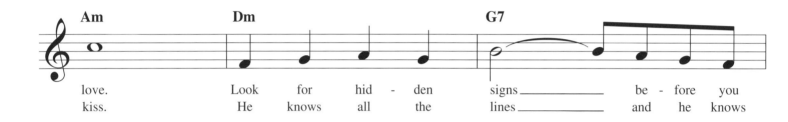

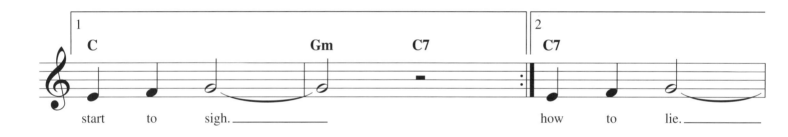

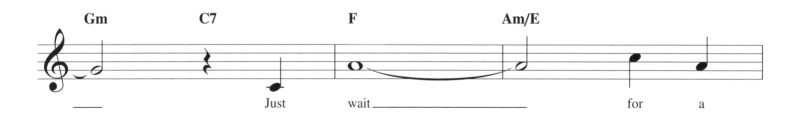

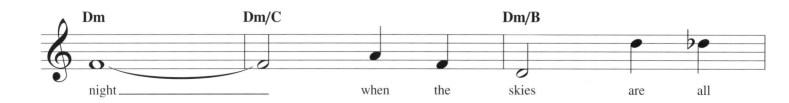

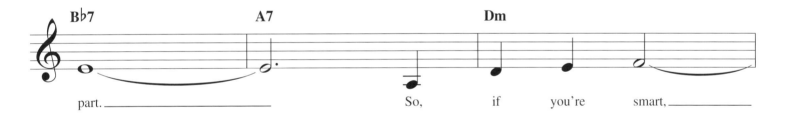
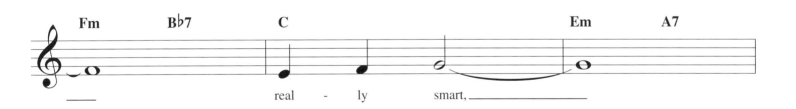

THE OTHER SIDE OF THE TRACKS
from LITTLE ME

Music by CY COLEMAN
Lyrics by CAROLYN LEIGH

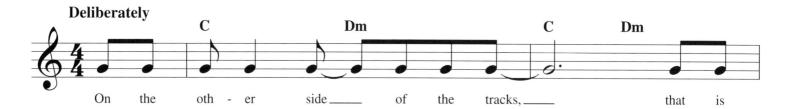
On the oth-er side of the tracks, that is

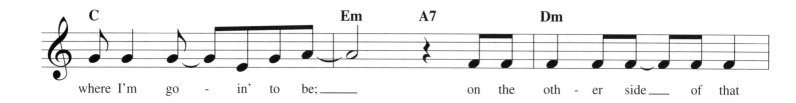
where I'm go-in' to be; on the oth-er side of that

great di-vide, be-tween fame and for-tune and me! Gon-na

put my shad-ows be-hind me. Give my in-hi-bi-tions the

axe; and to-mor-row morn-ing you'll find me, on the oth-er side of the

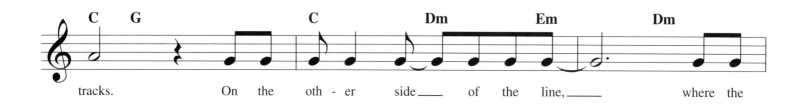
tracks. On the oth-er side of the line, where the

life is fan-cy and free, gon-na sit and fan on my

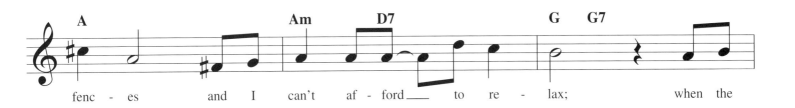
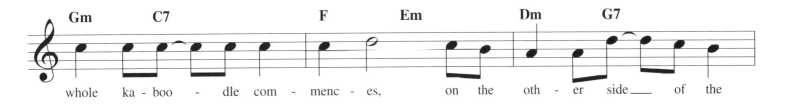

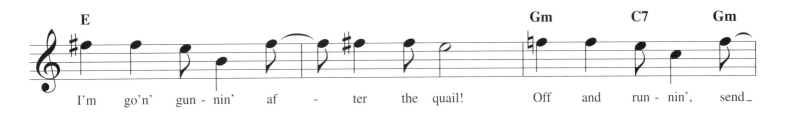

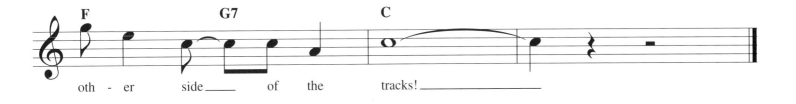

OUT OF NOWHERE
from the Paramount Picture DUDE RANCH

Words by EDWARD HEYMAN
Music by JOHNNY GREEN

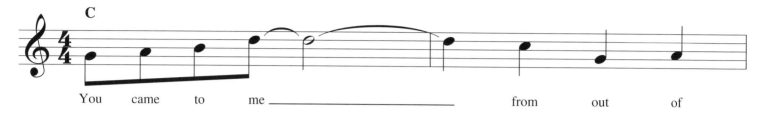
You came to me from out of

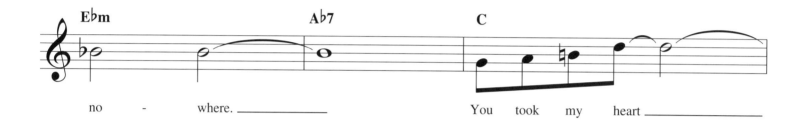
no - where. You took my heart

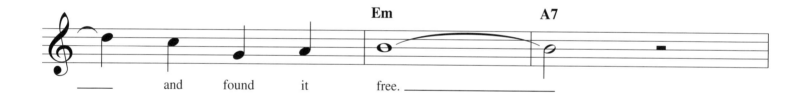
and found it free.

Won - der - ful dreams, won - der - ful schemes from no -

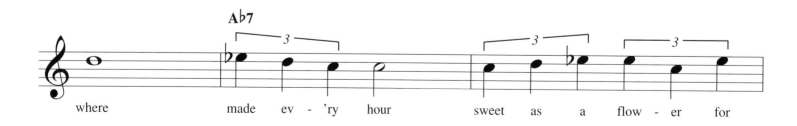
where made ev - 'ry hour sweet as a flow - er for

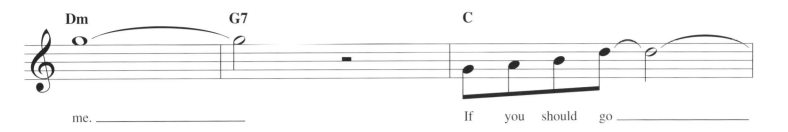

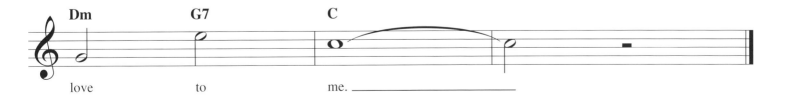

PICK YOURSELF UP
from SWING TIME

Words by DOROTHY FIELDS
Music by JEROME KERN

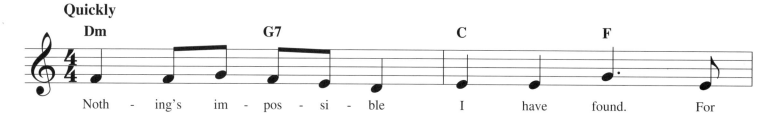
Noth-ing's im-pos-si-ble I have found. For

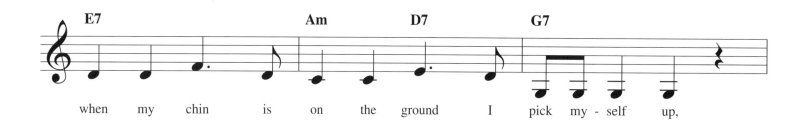
when my chin is on the ground I pick my-self up,

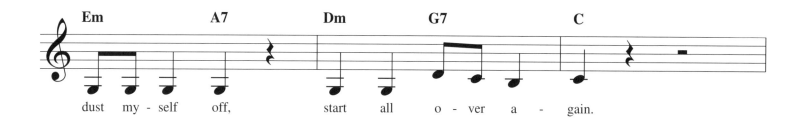
dust my-self off, start all o-ver a-gain.

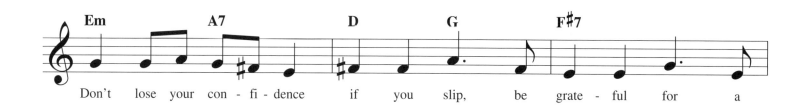
Don't lose your con-fi-dence if you slip, be grate-ful for a

pleas-ant trip, and pick your-self up, dust your-self off,

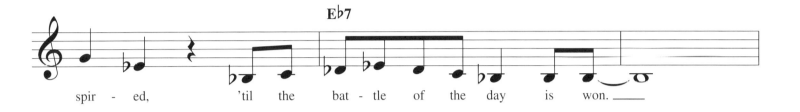

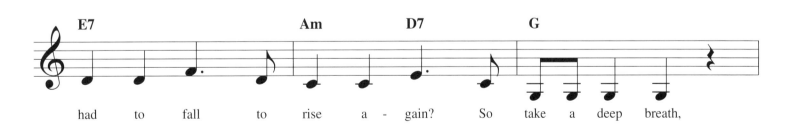
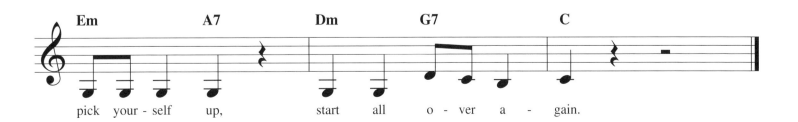

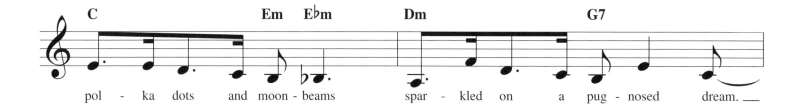

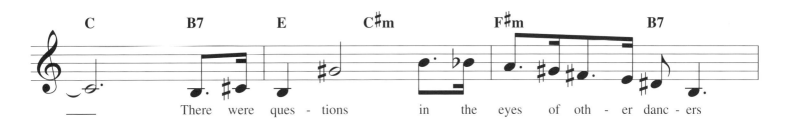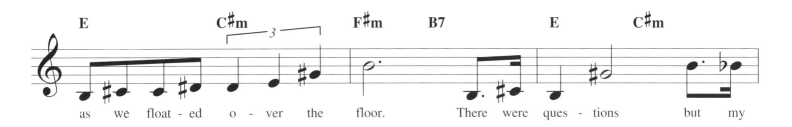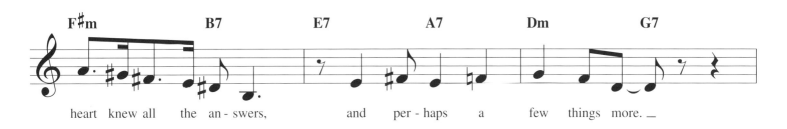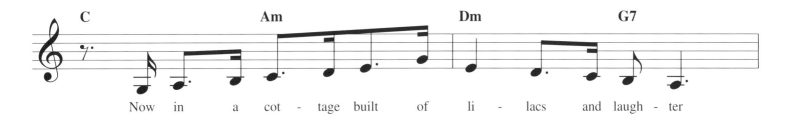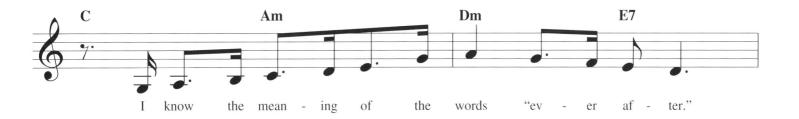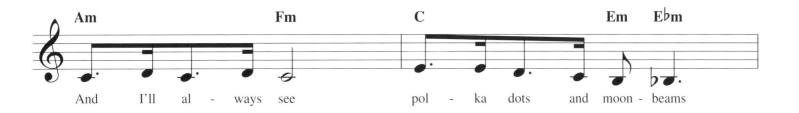

PRELUDE TO A KISS

Words by IRVING GORDON and IRVING MILLS
Music by DUKE ELLINGTON

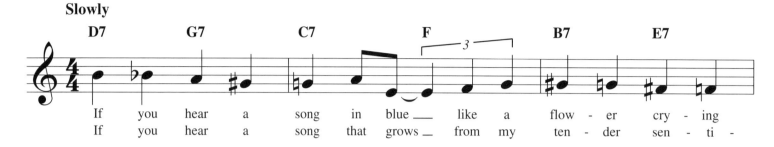

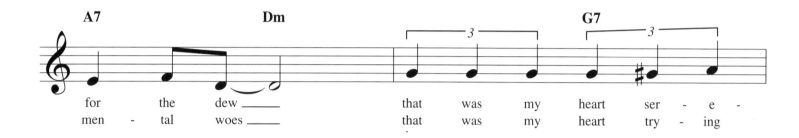

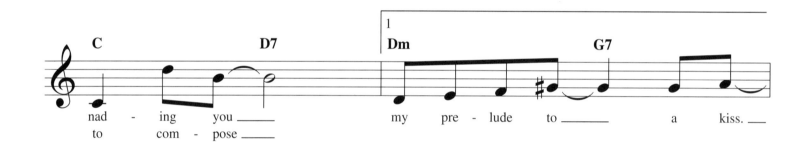

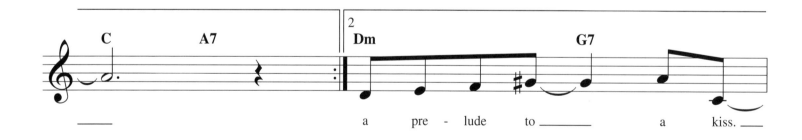

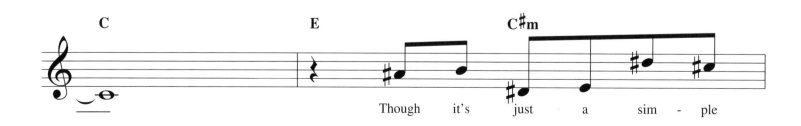

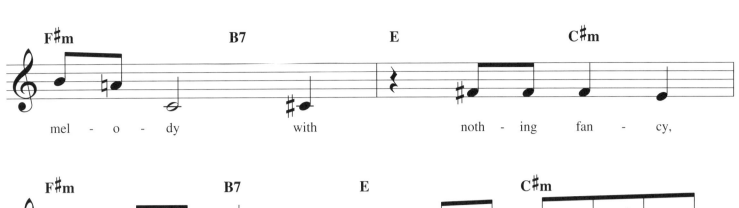
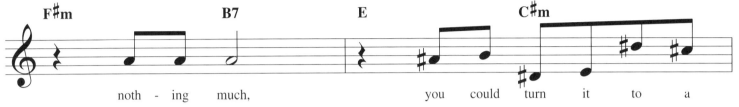

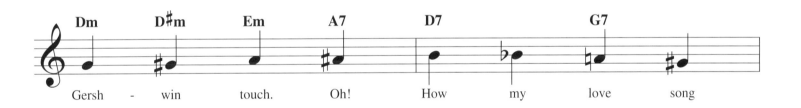
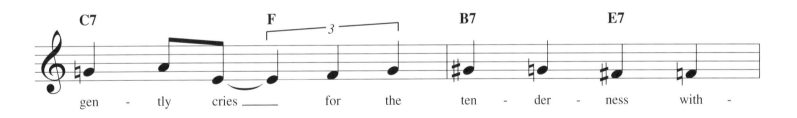
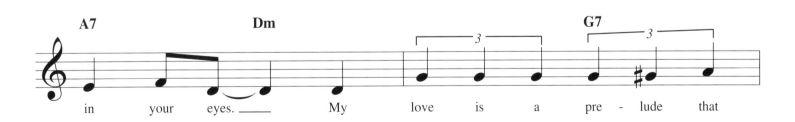
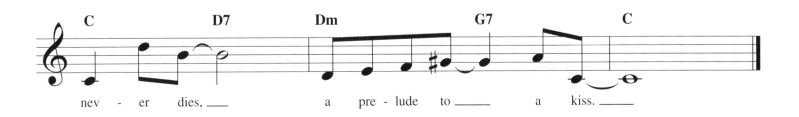

QUIET NIGHTS OF QUIET STARS
(Corcovado)

English Words by GENE LEES
Original Words and Music by ANTONIO CARLOS JOBIM

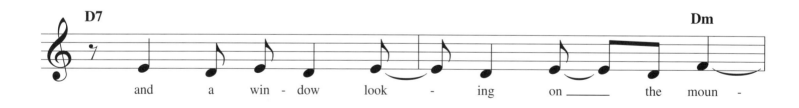

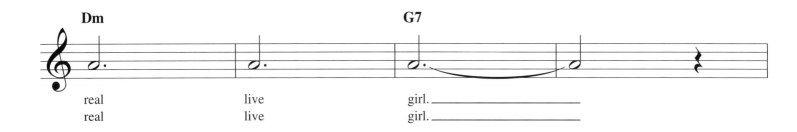

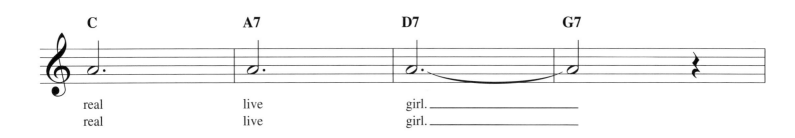

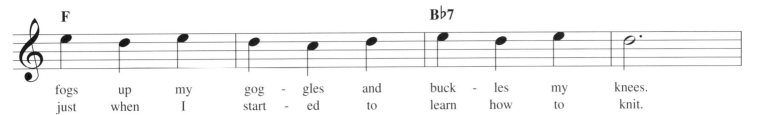
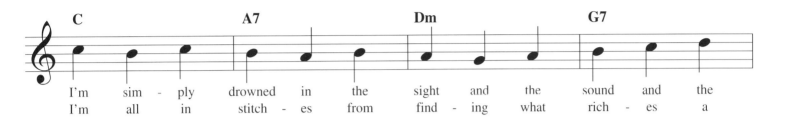
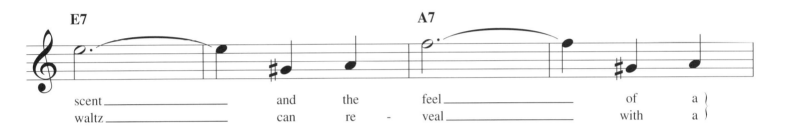
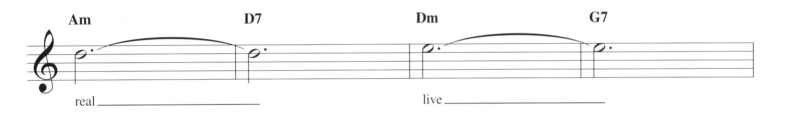
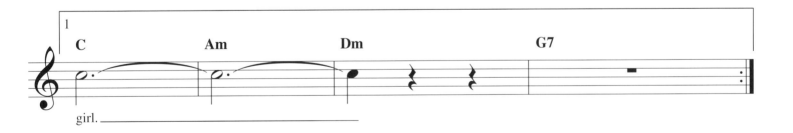
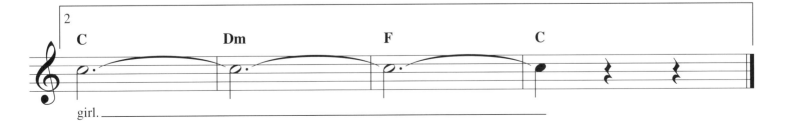

SHALL WE DANCE?
from THE KING AND I

Lyrics by OSCAR HAMMERSTEIN II
Music by RICHARD RODGERS

Shall we dance? On a bright cloud of

mu - sic shall we fly? Shall we

dance? Shall we then say "good-

night" and mean "good-bye?" Or, per-

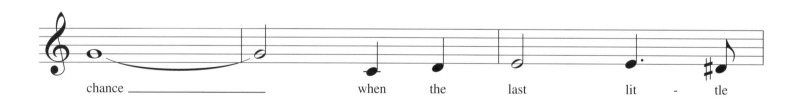
chance when the last lit - tle

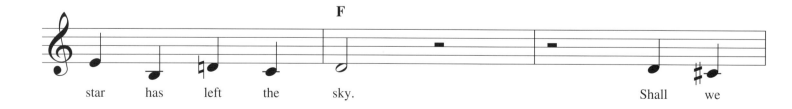
star has left the sky. Shall we

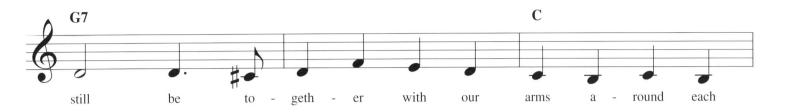
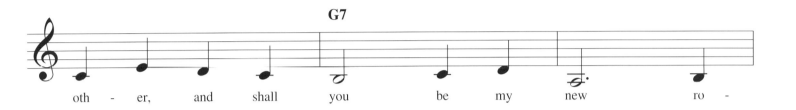
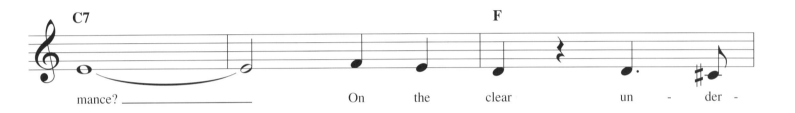
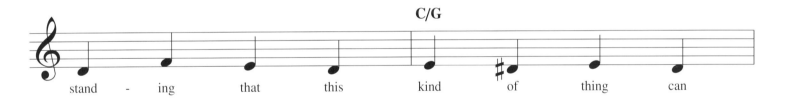
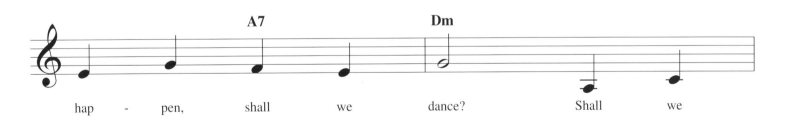
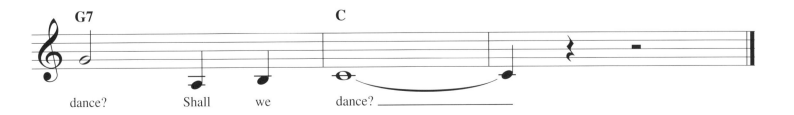

SO NICE
(Summer Samba)

Original Words and Music by MARCOS VALLE
and PAULO SERGIO VALLE
English Words by NORMAN GIMBEL

Some-one to hold me tight, that would be ver-y nice,

some-one to love me right, that would be ver-y nice.

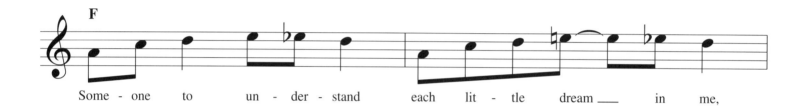
Some-one to un-der-stand each lit-tle dream in me,

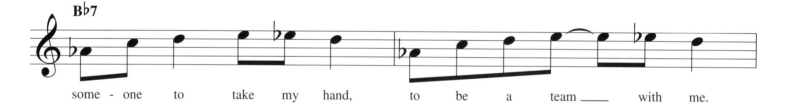
some-one to take my hand, to be a team with me.

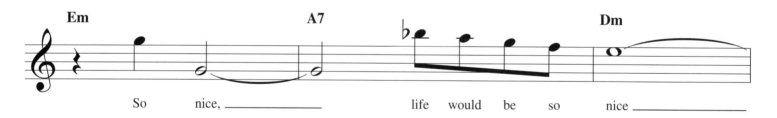
So nice, life would be so nice

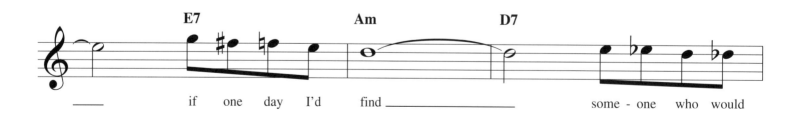
if one day I'd find some-one who would

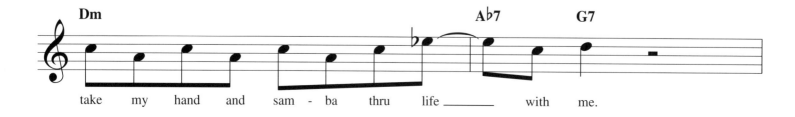
take my hand and sam-ba thru life with me.

165

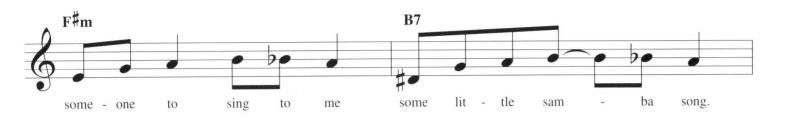
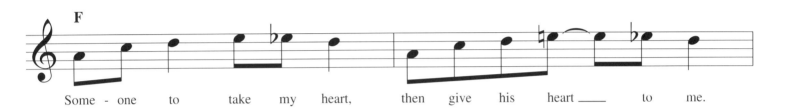
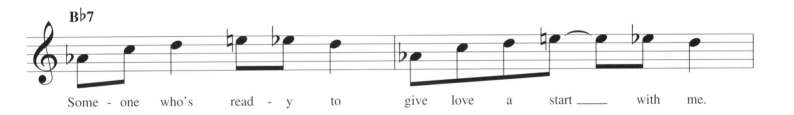
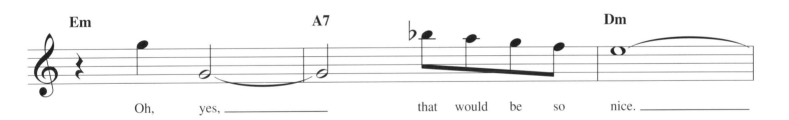

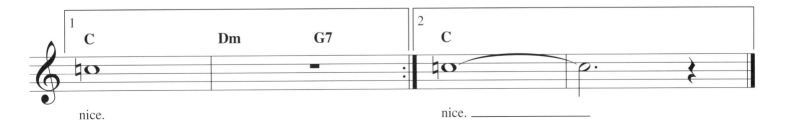

A Sunday Kind of Love

TIME AFTER TIME
from the Metro-Goldwyn-Mayer Picture IT HAPPENED IN BROOKLYN

Words by SAMMY CAHN
Music by JULE STYNE

Copyright © 1947 (Renewed) Sands Music Corp.
All Rights Reserved Used by Permission

Moderately

Time af-ter time I tell my-self that I'm so

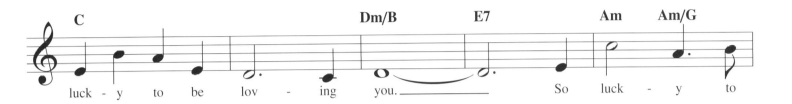
luck-y to be lov-ing you. So luck-y to

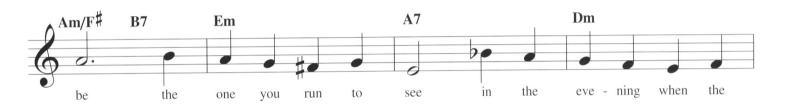
be the one you run to see in the eve-ning when the

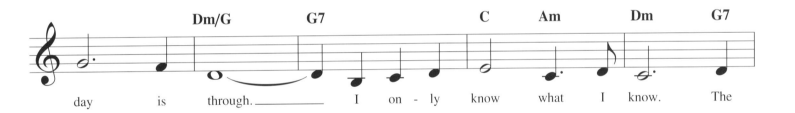
day is through. I on-ly know what I know. The

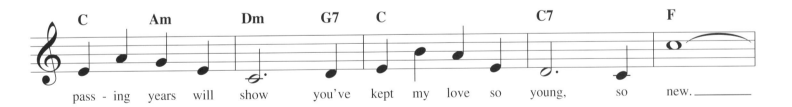
pass-ing years will show you've kept my love so young, so new.

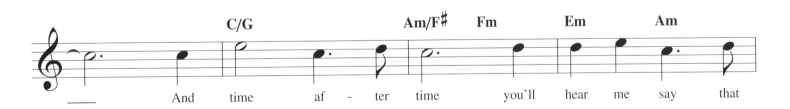
And time af-ter time you'll hear me say that

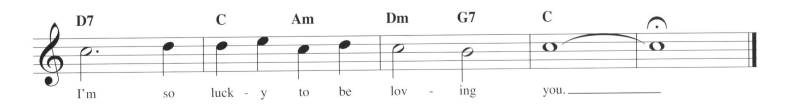
I'm so luck-y to be lov-ing you.

THE SURREY WITH THE FRINGE ON TOP
from OKLAHOMA!

Lyrics by OSCAR HAMMERSTEIN II
Music by RICHARD RODGERS

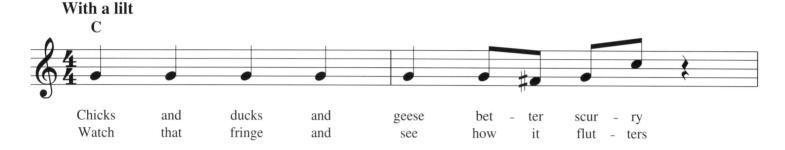
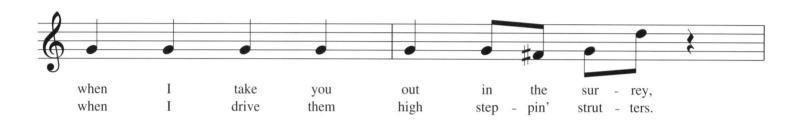
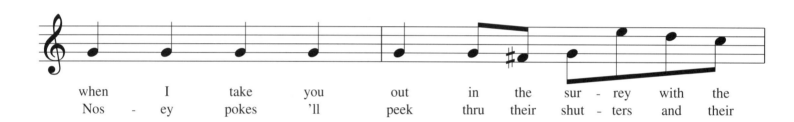
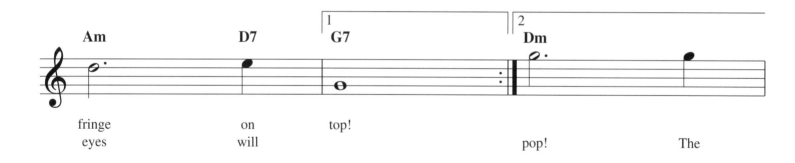

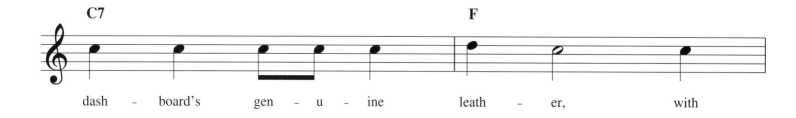

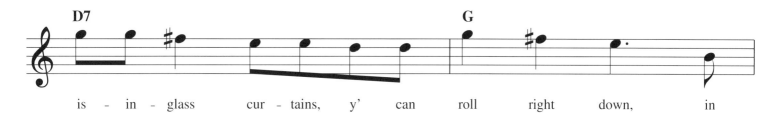
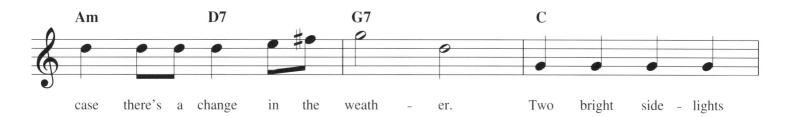

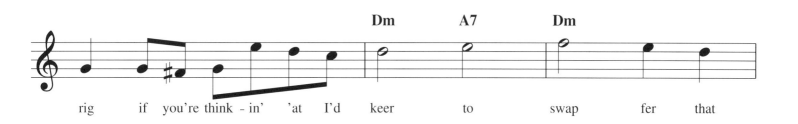
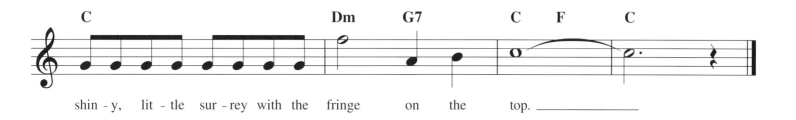

THERE WILL NEVER BE ANOTHER YOU
from the Motion Picture ICELAND

Lyric by MACK GORDON
Music by HARRY WARREN

© 1942 (Renewed) TWENTIETH CENTURY MUSIC CORPORATION
All Rights Controlled by MORLEY MUSIC CO.
All Rights Reserved

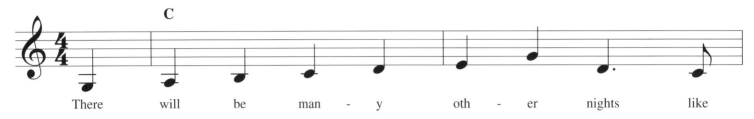
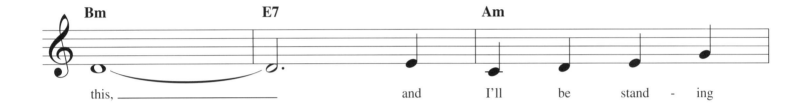
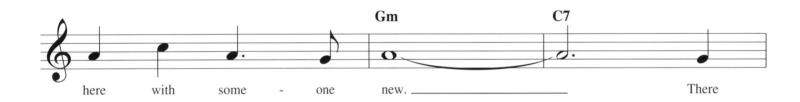
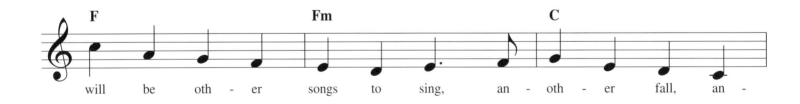

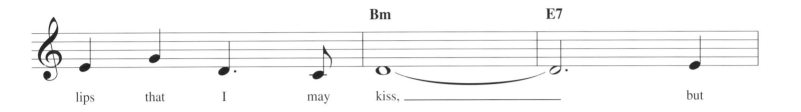

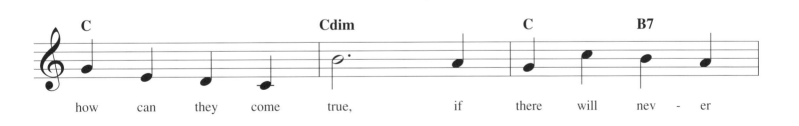
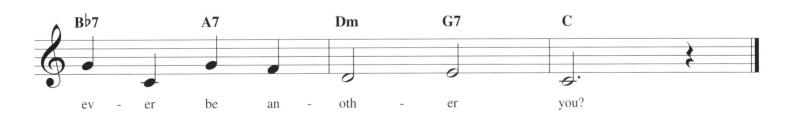

Up with the Lark

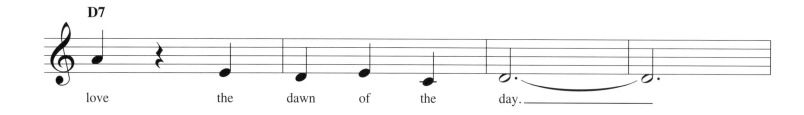
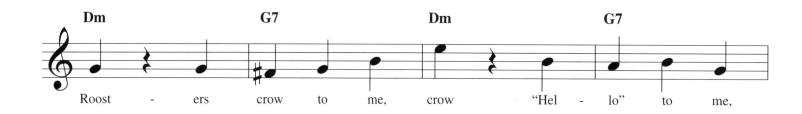

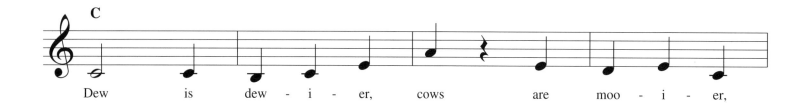
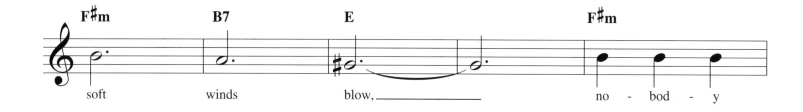

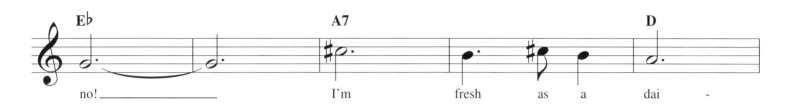
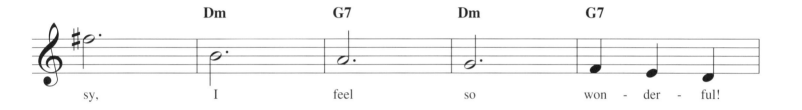

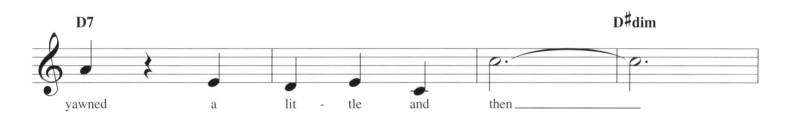
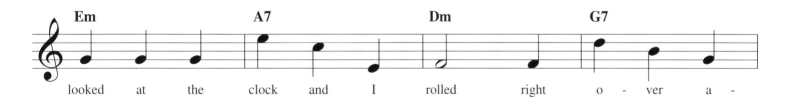

THE WAY YOU LOOK TONIGHT
from SWING TIME

Words by DOROTHY FIELDS
Music by JEROME KERN

Moderately

Some - day when I'm aw - f'ly low,
love - ly, with your smile so warm
Love - ly, nev - er, nev - er change,

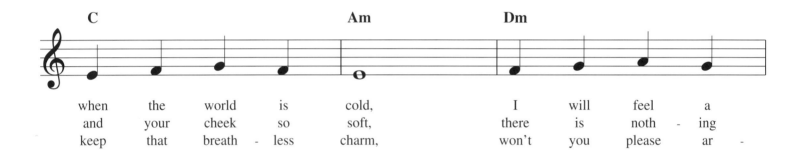

when the world is cold, I will feel a
and your cheek so soft, there is nothing
keep that breath - less charm, won't you please ar -

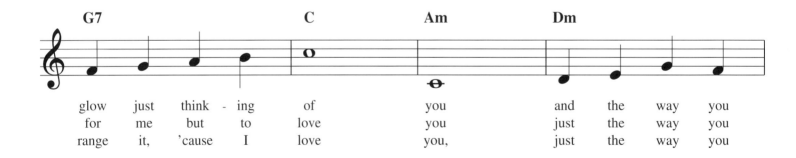

glow just think - ing of you and the way you
for me but to love you just the way you
range it, 'cause I love you, just the way you

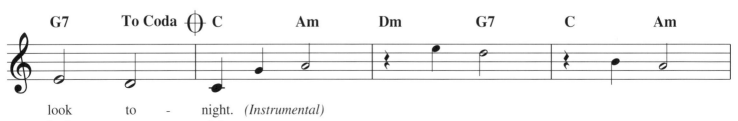

look to - night. *(Instrumental)*
look to - night.
look to -

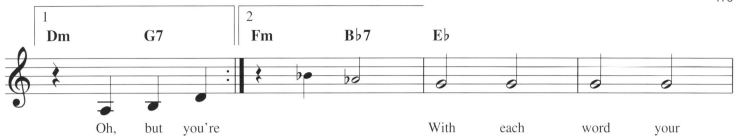
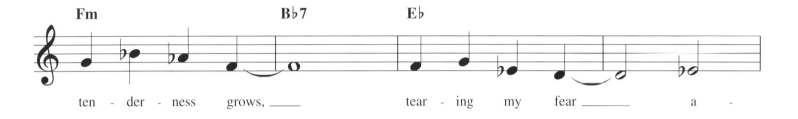
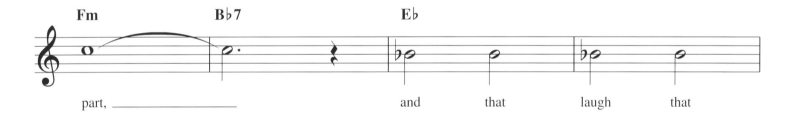
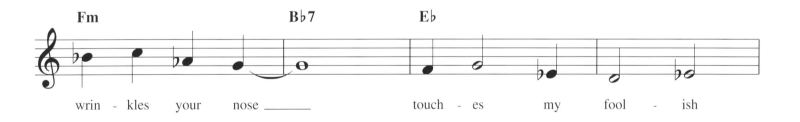
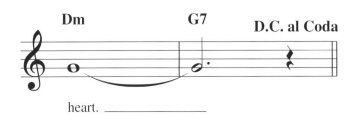

WITCHCRAFT

Music by CY COLEMAN
Lyrics by CAROLYN LEIGH

© 1957 MORLEY MUSIC CO.
Copyright Renewed and Assigned to MORLEY MUSIC CO.
and NOTABLE MUSIC COMPANY, INC.
All Rights for NOTABLE MUSIC COMPANY, INC. Administered by CHRYSALIS MUSIC
All Rights Reserved   Used by Permission

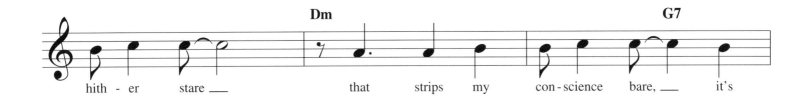

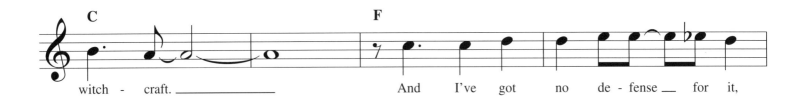

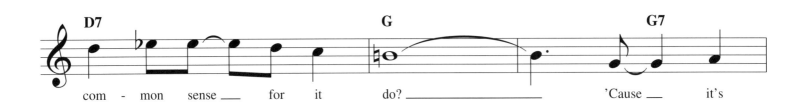

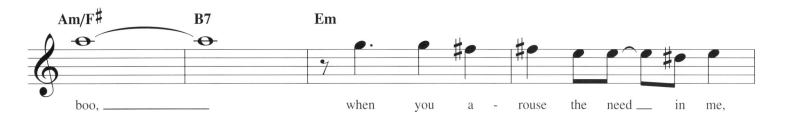

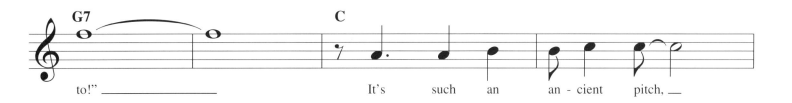
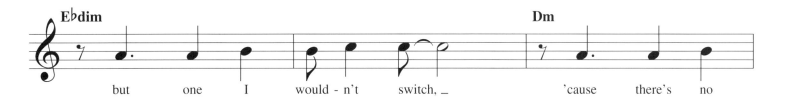
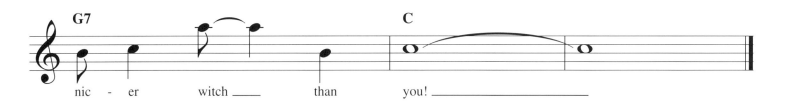

WIVES AND LOVERS
(Hey, Little Girl)
from the Paramount Picture WIVES AND LOVERS

Words by HAL DAVID
Music by BURT BACHARACH

Moderately fast

Hey, little girl, comb your hair, fix your make-up, soon he will o-pen the door.
Day af-ter day there are girls at the of-fice and men will al-ways be men.

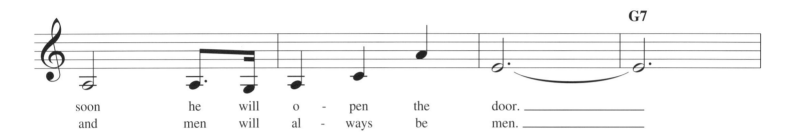

Don't think be-cause there's a ring on your fin-ger you need-n't try an-y-more. For
Don't send him off with your hair still in curl-ers, you may not see him a-gain. For

wives should al-ways be lov-ers too.
wives should al-ways be lov-ers too.

Run to his arms the mo-ment he comes home to
Run to his arms the mo-ment he comes home to

WRAP YOUR TROUBLES IN DREAMS
(And Dream Your Troubles Away)

Lyric by TED KOEHLER and BILLY MOLL
Music by HARRY BARRIS

Copyright © 1931 Shapiro, Bernstein & Co., Inc., New York,
  Fred Ahlert Music Group and Ted Koehler Music Co.
Copyright Renewed
All rights for Fred Ahlert Music Group and Ted Koehler Music Co. Administered by Bug Music
International Copyright Secured   All Rights Reserved
Used by Permission

Moderately slow

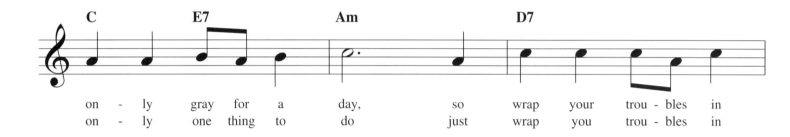
When skies are cloud-y and gray, they're
til that sun-shine peeps thru, there's

on-ly gray for a day, so wrap your trou-bles in
on-ly one thing to do just wrap you trou-bles in

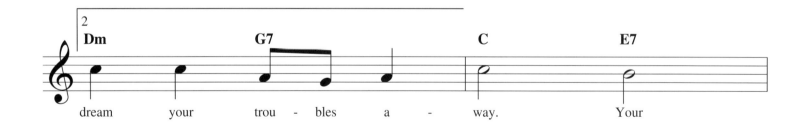
1. dreams and dream your trou-bles a-way. Un-
   dreams and

2. dream your trou-bles a-way. Your

cas-tles may tum-ble, that's Fate, af-ter all,

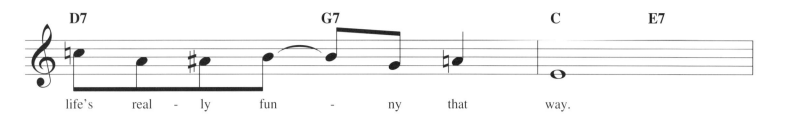
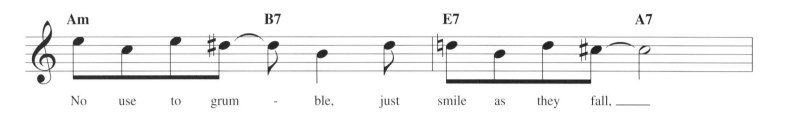

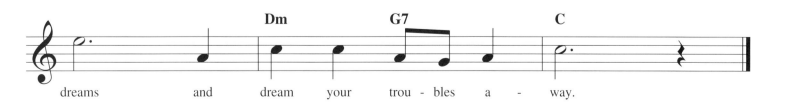

YOU ARE TOO BEAUTIFUL
from HALLELUJAH, I'M A BUM

Words by LORENZ HART
Music by RICHARD RODGERS

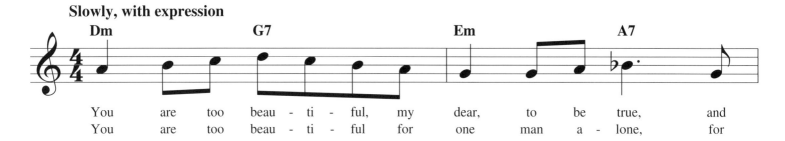

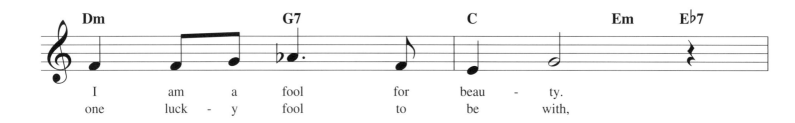

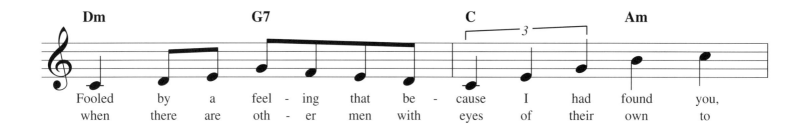

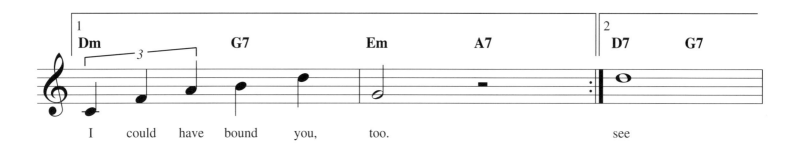

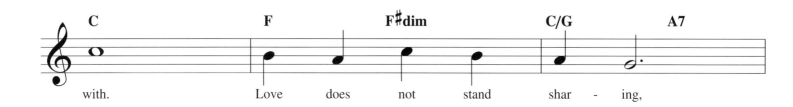

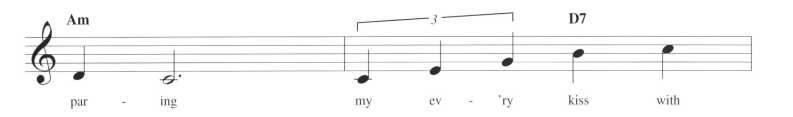
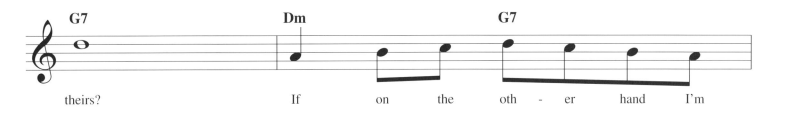
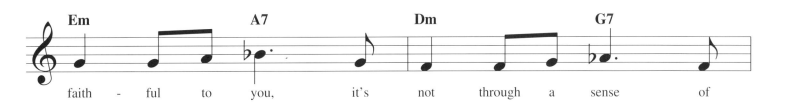
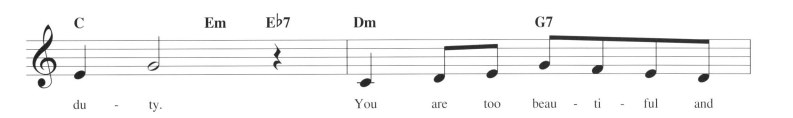
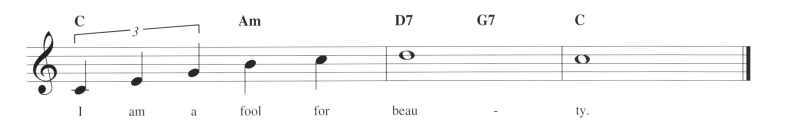

YOU BROUGHT A NEW KIND OF LOVE TO ME

from the Paramount Picture THE BIG POND
from NEW YORK, NEW YORK

Words and Music by SAMMY FAIN,
IRVING KAHAL and PIERRE NORMAN

If the night-in-gales could sing like you, they'd

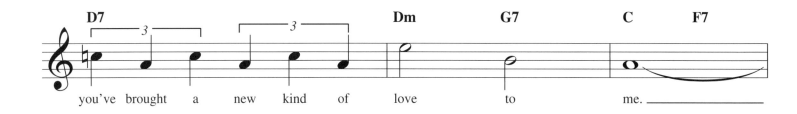

sing much sweet-er than they do, for

you've brought a new kind of love to me.

If the sand-man brought me dreams of you, I'd

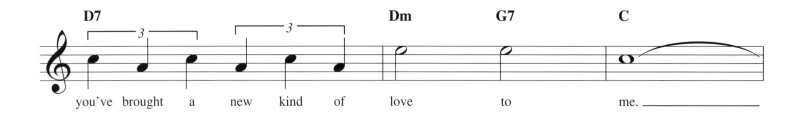

want to sleep my whole life through, for

you've brought a new kind of love to me.

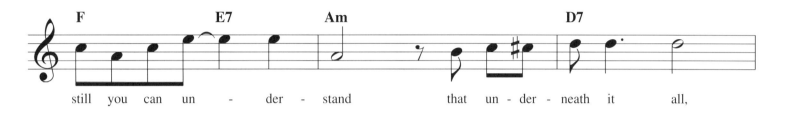

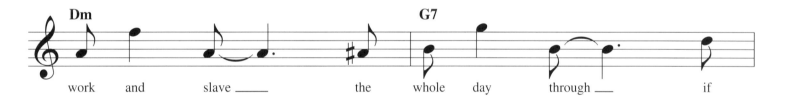

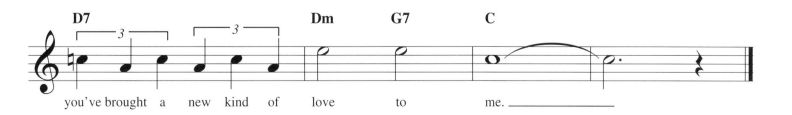

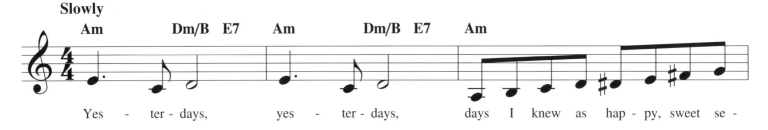

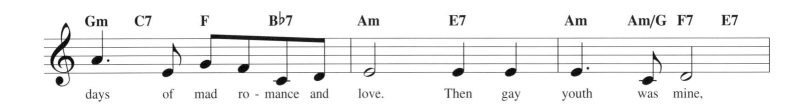

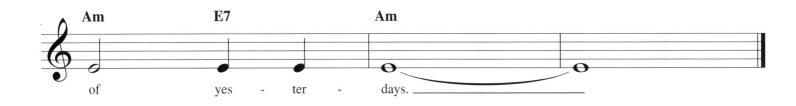

CHORD SPELLER

C chords			C♯ or D♭ chords			D chords	
C	C–E–G		C♯	C♯–F–G♯		D	D–F♯–A
Cm	C–E♭–G		C♯m	C♯–E–G♯		Dm	D–F–A
C7	C–E–G–B♭		C♯7	C♯–F–G♯–B		D7	D–F♯–A–C
Cdim	C–E♭–G♭		C♯dim	C♯–E–G		Ddim	D–F–A♭
C+	C–E–G♯		C♯+	C♯–F–A		D+	D–F♯–A♯

E♭ chords			E chords			F chords	
E♭	E♭–G–B♭		E	E–G♯–B		F	F–A–C
E♭m	E♭–G♭–B♭		Em	E–G–B		Fm	F–A♭–C
E♭7	E♭–G–B♭–D♭		E7	E–G♯–B–D		F7	F–A–C–E♭
E♭dim	E♭–G♭–A		Edim	E–G–B♭		Fdim	F–A♭–B
E♭+	E♭–G–B		E+	E–G♯–C		F+	F–A–C♯

F♯ or G♭ chords			G chords			G♯ or A♭ chords	
F♯	F♯–A♯–C♯		G	G–B–D		A♭	A♭–C–E♭
F♯m	F♯–A–C♯		Gm	G–B♭–D		A♭m	A♭–B–E♭
F♯7	F♯–A♯–C♯–E		G7	G–B–D–F		A♭7	A♭–C–E♭–G♭
F♯dim	F♯–A–C		Gdim	G–B♭–D♭		A♭dim	A♭–B–D
F♯+	F♯–A♯–D		G+	G–B–D♯		A♭+	A♭–C–E

A chords			B♭ chords			B chords	
A	A–C♯–E		B♭	B♭–D–F		B	B–D♯–F♯
Am	A–C–E		B♭m	B♭–D♭–F		Bm	B–D–F♯
A7	A–C♯–E–G		B♭7	B♭–D–F–A♭		B7	B–D♯–F♯–A
Adim	A–C–E♭		B♭dim	B♭–D♭–E		Bdim	B–D–F
A+	A–C♯–F		B♭+	B♭–D–F♯		B+	B–D♯–G

Important Note: A slash chord (C/E, G/B) tells you that a certain bass note is to be played under a particular harmony. In the case of C/E, the chord is C and the bass note is E.

THE ULTIMATE FAKE BOOK
4TH EDITION

Nearly two decades ago, Hal Leonard created *The Ultimate Fake Book*, a collection of more than 1,200 songs which lived up to its name and set the standard for all fake books that followed. Recently, we created a new collection intended to update and improve upon *The Ultimate Fake Book* and offer musicians the most incredible selection of songs in one collection. Simply called *The Book*, it included the very best songs from *The Ultimate Fake Book* plus even more classic and current tunes. After many years, *The Ultimate Fake Book* has gone out of print and *The Book* has now been retitled *The Ultimate Fake Book, Fourth Edition*. It is truly the best standard fake book available ... period. We invite you to once again experience *The Ultimate!*

SONGS INCLUDE: Alfie • All I Ask of You • All the Things You Are • Always • And So It Goes • Autumn in New York • Beauty and the Beast • Blue Skies • Body and Soul • Call Me Irresponsible • Can't Help Falling in Love • Candy • Caravan • Cry Me a River • Duke of Earl • Easter Parade • Endless Love • Fields of Gold • Got to Get You into My Life • Heart and Soul • Here's That Rainy Day • How Deep Is the Ocean (How High Is the Sky) • I Got a Woman • I Love Paris • I Shot the Sheriff • I'm Always Chasing Rainbows • I've Got the World on a String • The Impossible Dream • Isn't It Romantic? • It's Only a Paper Moon • Kisses Sweeter than Wine • The Lady Is a Tramp • Lay Down Sally • Let's Fall in Love • Little Girl Blue • Love Is Just Around the Corner • Lullaby of the Leaves • Makin' Whoopee! • Memory • Midnight Train to Georgia • Mona Lisa • Moon River • Moonlight in Vermont • My Funny Valentine • Nights in White Satin • On the Street Where You Live • Operator • Paperback Writer • Piano Man • Precious and Few • Puttin' on the Ritz • Return to Sender • Roxanne • Satin Doll • Sh-Boom (Life Could Be a Dream) • Shake, Rattle and Roll • Shout • Small World • Some Day My Prince Will Come • Somewhere Out There • Sophisticated Lady • Speak Low • Speak Softly, Love (Love Theme from *The Godfather*) • Splish Splash • Stand by Me • Strawberry Fields Forever • Tears in Heaven • Ticket to Ride • A Time for Us (Love Theme from *Romeo & Juliet*) • Unforgettable • Waltz for Debby • What Now My Love • What'll I Do • When I Fall in Love • When You Wish Upon a Star • and hundreds more!

00240024	C Edition	**$49.95**
00240025	E♭ Edition	**$49.95**
00240026	B♭ Edition	**$49.95**

Prices, contents, and availability subject to change without notice.

There is no song duplication between **THE ULTIMATE FAKE BOOK** and **THE BEST FAKE BOOK EVER!**

FOR MORE INFORMATION, SEE YOUR LOCAL MUSIC DEALER, OR WRITE TO:

HAL•LEONARD CORPORATION
7777 W. BLUEMOUND RD. P.O. BOX 13819 MILWAUKEE, WI 53213

THE EASY FAKE BOOK SERIES

100 songs from your favorite decades of music

This series of beginning fake books for players new to "faking" includes:
- 100 memorable songs, all in the key of C
- Lyrics
- Chords which have been simplified, but remain true to each tune
- Easy-to-read, large music notation

THE EASY FORTIES FAKE BOOK

This '40s edition includes: Ac-cent-Tchu-ate the Positive • The Anniversary Waltz • Be Careful, It's My Heart • Bésame Mucho (Kiss Me Much) • Bewitched • Boogie Woogie Bugle Boy • Come Rain or Come Shine • Don't Get Around Much Anymore • Easy Street • Frenesí • Harlem Nocturne • Have I Told You Lately That I Love You • How High the Moon • I Got It Bad and That Ain't Good • I'll Remember April • I'm Beginning to See the Light • It Could Happen to You • Java Jive • Love Letters • Mairzy Doats • Moonlight in Vermont • A Nightingale Sang in Berkeley Square • On a Slow Boat to China • Sentimental Journey • Stella by Starlight • The Surrey with the Fringe on Top • Tangerine • You'd Be So Nice to Come Home To • You're Nobody 'til Somebody Loves You • and dozens more.
00240252 Melody/Lyrics/Chords..$19.95

THE EASY FIFTIES FAKE BOOK

Includes: All I Have to Do Is Dream • At the Hop • Beyond the Sea • Blueberry Hill • Chantilly Lace • Don't Be Cruel (To a Heart That's True) • Dream Lover • Earth Angel • Great Balls of Fire • Heartbreak Hotel • Jambalaya (On the Bayou) • Kansas City • La Bamba • Love and Marriage • Love Me Tender • Magic Moments • Mister Sandman • Mona Lisa • Peggy Sue • Put Your Head on My Shoulder • Que Sera, Sera (Whatever Will Be, Will Be) • Rock Around the Clock • Sea of Love • Sh-Boom (Life Could Be a Dream) • Sixteen Candles • Smoke Gets in Your Eyes • Splish Splash • Tennessee Waltz • Unchained Melody • You Belong to Me • Your Cheatin' Heart • and dozens more.
00240255 Melody/Lyrics/Chords..$19.95

THE EASY SIXTIES FAKE BOOK

100 songs from the '60s: Along Comes Mary • Baby Love • Barbara Ann • Born to Be Wild • Brown Eyed Girl • California Girls • Call Me • Dancing in the Street • Do Wah Diddy Diddy • Do You Know the Way to San Jose • The Girl from Ipanema • Good Vibrations • A Groovy Kind of Love • Happy Together • Hey Jude • I Can't Help Myself (Sugar Pie, Honey Bunch) • I Heard It Through the Grapevine • Leader of the Pack • Leaving on a Jet Plane • Louie, Louie • Magic Carpet Ride • Moon River • Respect • (Sittin' On) The Dock of the Bay • Soul Man • Strangers in the Night • Sweet Caroline • Turn! Turn! Turn! • The Twist • Yesterday • and more.
00240253 Melody/Lyrics/Chords..$19.95

THE EASY SEVENTIES FAKE BOOK

Songs from the '70s edition include: Ain't No Mountain High Enough • American Pie • Angie • Baby, I Love Your Way • Bad, Bad Leroy Brown • The Boys Are Back in Town • Come Sail Away • Crocodile Rock • Drift Away • Fame • Free Bird • Honesty • I Will Survive • I'll Never Love This Way Again • Joy to the World • Let It Be • Rainy Days and Mondays • Reeling in the Years • She Believes in Me • Stayin' Alive • Take a Chance on Me • Take Me Home, Country Roads • We Are the Champions • Wonderful Tonight • Y.M.C.A. • You Are So Beautiful • You've Got a Friend • dozens more.
00240256 Melody/Lyrics/Chords..$19.95

Visit Hal Leonard online at **www.halleonard.com** for complete songlists and more.

For More Information, See Your Local Music Dealer,
Or Write To:

HAL•LEONARD® CORPORATION
7777 W. BLUEMOUND RD. P.O. BOX 13819 MILWAUKEE, WI 53213

Prices, contents and availability subject to change without notice.